ALSO BY CAMONGHNE FELIX

Dyscalculia
Build Yourself a Boat

LET THE POETS GOVERN

LET THE POETS GOVERN

A DECLARATION OF FREEDOM

CAMONGHNE FELIX

ONE WORLD - NEW YORK

One World
An imprint of Random House
A division of Penguin Random House LLC
1745 Broadway, New York, NY 10019
oneworldlit.com
penguinrandomhouse.com
Copyright © 2026 by Camonghne Felix

Penguin Random House values and supports copyright. Copyright fuels creativity, encourages diverse voices, promotes free speech, and creates a vibrant culture. Thank you for buying an authorized edition of this book and for complying with copyright laws by not reproducing, scanning, or distributing any part of it in any form without permission. You are supporting writers and allowing Penguin Random House to continue to publish books for every reader. Please note that no part of this book may be used or reproduced in any manner for the purpose of training artificial intelligence technologies or systems.

ONE WORLD and colophon are registered trademarks of Penguin Random House LLC.

Facebook comments reprinted with the permission of Kiese Laymon. The poem "Callaloo" is reprinted from *Because the Dawn Breaks!: Poems Dedicated to the Grenadian People* with the permission of Merle Collins. The poem "The perplexing smiles of the children of Palestine" by Marcellus "Khaliifah" Williams is reprinted from *Tempest Mag* with the permission of *Tempest Mag*. The poem can be found at tempestmag.org/2024/10/the-perplexing-smiles-of-the-children-of-palestine/.

LIBRARY OF CONGRESS CATALOGING-IN-PUBLICATION DATA
Names: Felix, Camonghne author
Title: Let the poets govern / by Camonghne Felix.
Description: New York, NY : One World, 2026.
Identifiers: LCCN 2025036305 (print) | LCCN 2025036306 (ebook) | ISBN 9780593242148 hardcover | ISBN 9780593242155 ebook
Subjects: LCSH: Felix, Camonghne | African American poets—Biography | Speechwriters—United States—Biography | American poetry—African American authors—History and criticism | Political poetry, American—History and criticism | LCGFT: Autobiographies | Literary criticism
Classification: LCC PS3606.E3879 Z46 2026 (print) | LCC PS3606.E3879 (ebook)
LC record available at https://lccn.loc.gov/2025036305
LC ebook record available at https://lccn.loc.gov/2025036306

Printed in the United States of America on acid-free paper

1st Printing

First Edition

BOOK TEAM: Production editor: Loren Noveck • Managing editor: Rebecca Berlant • Production manager: Mark Maguire • Copy editor: Emily DeHuff • Proofreaders: Janet Renard, Adele Starrs, and Olivia Trzaski

Book design by Edwin Vazquez

The authorized representative in the EU for product safety and compliance is Penguin Random House Ireland, Morrison Chambers, 32 Nassau Street, Dublin D02 YH68, Ireland. https://eu-contact.penguin.ie

For Snowy, my father

This is an offering to the ones in violent flight from the militarized enclosure of politics out into the social life that surrounds it, which is where we are and what we were all along.
—Fred Moten and Stefano Harney

What a poet does, ideally, is talk about the history of the inside of people so that history is more than just the appearance of things.
—Lucille Clifton

CONTENTS

PRELUDE		3
CHAPTER 1:	**THE INTRODUCTION**	9
CHAPTER 2:	**THE LULLABY AND THE NURSERY RHYME**	21
CHAPTER 3:	**THE PLEDGE**	43
CHAPTER 4:	**THE SUGAR**	63
CHAPTER 5:	**THE ORDER**	94
CHAPTER 6:	**THE SPIRITUAL**	108
CHAPTER 7:	**THE POLITICS OF NOW**	123
CHAPTER 8:	**THE OLIVE SEASON**	148
CHAPTER 9:	**THE FOURTH SERMON ON THE WARPLANE, OR THE CODA**	168
ACKNOWLEDGMENTS		177

LET THE POETS GOVERN

PRELUDE

Poets have been writing about the ending, and its child, eternity, for all of time. We are at the end of the long tail of the end, and you can taste the anguish in the air. We are apologizing to our offspring for the failure of our foresight—we thought we'd see the end only from our graves. It was a foolish assumption, given that the destruction and desecration of all that is precious on the earth are happening in our time and on our watch. Finally, the end has come upon us like a lid sliding across the mouth of a canyon.

The poet saw this coming. The poet divines. The poet witnesses our ignorance and tells us about the material and spiritual power of language, that which shapes our reality. The poet tells us the truest stories about who we are. The poet isn't inherently good or bad, the poet isn't a god, the poet is a reflection of what surrounds her.

I knew early on that I would be a poet. My instinct has always been to document my life and the universe that I'd entered so that this documentation could help me understand how to see. My sight had long been filtered through the rose-colored lens of democracy, until Aiyana, then Trayvon. Then Eric and Walter, Freddie and Alton. Every time there was a new name, God felt more obscure, more impossible. And once that faith was gone, what else was there to believe in? I had seen a boy close to my own age slain in his own blood, and a little girl stained in hers. I learned about it all as I watched the evening news with my mother and realized that this barbarity was directed at us, at me.

To understand how we arrived here, at this time, right now, is to understand the most insidious side of humanness: We crafted a genius manipulation tactic—language. We are all born to be poets. We are all born with the ability to absorb and experience the details of our days—the light graze of a summer breeze, the tongue tasting complexity—and to transfigure those details into images that tell stories about how we live and who we are. But there are poets who have cast themselves as the victors of language, who have used language as a way to envision and invent a future in which they are the owners of comfort and safety. In which they distribute it to whoever they have decided most deserves it. They take the neutrality of poetry and sully its blank slate with frenzied terror.

Poetry is an act, and some of us have used poetry to act against poetry's best impulses.

I write this book to tell you a story about how the legal documents of yesterday, written by those who used language to conjure a world where only they had power, have shaped the world of today. This book is about how the poetics of the past became the material of the future. It is about how the poem has functioned throughout time, how the poem collects data, and how the poem organizes that data to tell us something about history that we'd never known. It is about rejecting a language that seeks to obliterate those of us who need language the most.

There are consequences for the way we've used language to harm. Consequences for using language to exploit. We are witnessing, in real time, the consequences of weaponizing language for the benefit of capital. When the language is toxic, we hurt. When the language is healthy, we thrive. Language has no morals or ethics, but it defines our morals and our ethics, and we have used it to establish the worst of our morals, the worst of our ethics. We have yet to truly articulate the best of what we could be.

Language evolves and takes many forms, but we standardize it, force it into assimilation. Take the English language, for instance, which has been forced into the mouths of more than one billion speakers, a language that has achieved dominance. It is a tool of coercion, a tool that forces on the speaker an established set of values, values that are then encoded into the documents that organize our society. Every document tasked with the responsibility of speaking for the many fails as soon as it is written. When a word is translated, meaning is lost. And between each translation, intent is lost. When we lose intent, we lose language's functionality: Intent is context. Intent is subtext.

The poem proves that to us again and again. Intent gives us the information we need in order to know what the poem really wants to say.

I use the erasure poem in this book as not just a literary tool, but a comment on the necessity of revision. By creating erasure poems out of legal documents that have designed the last six hundred years of humanity, I revisit the past and superimpose a new narrative, manipulate language in order to represent poetry's truest sense, the sense that turns language into a portal instead of a handshake. The erasure poem then becomes a way to enter, not only a way to be in touch. We cannot revise history but we can revise and redefine the language that governs history, the language that governs us.

The permission to be a poet is accessible to any of us. When we are kept away from that access, when that permission is withheld from us, we lose our relationship to the musicality of language, to a certain kind of intellect that our ancestors took care to cultivate. We lose our relationship to storytelling and our relationship to remembering. We lose the romance of being alive. We fall into the traps of solipsism and individualism, forgetting that interreliance is where our liberty lies. Each of us has the ability to see the world through a poet's eyes, the ability to find ourselves in a process of constant curiosity and creation, where what we want to see is made visible in real time. We all have it, and that "it" is the difference between an ending world and an endless world. The world we imagine is possible. Poetry allows us to trust that, to have faith in it, to see the impossible as possible. Poetry allows us to abstract the present in order to construct a new and unexpected future. It fractures—and deepens—time.

If the poet is in a state of rebellion from the expectations of form and history, she becomes fugitive. "It is not merely with his whole soul," Aimé Césaire—poet, politician, and hero of the negritude movement—says in his essay "Poetry and Knowledge," "it is with his entire being that the poet approaches the poem. What presides over the poem is not the most lucid intelligence, or the most acute sensibility, but an entire experience."* Poetry is the most radical representation of fugitivity because it's learned through a fugitive education—an education that cannot be taught in a classroom alone, not in the way mathematics is taught or the way the sciences can be taught. Certain forms like sonnets or ghazels have rules that require the poet to practice constraint. But when the poet breaks out of that constraint and challenges the rules, she remakes the form into something else. The poem insists on fugitivity—at once constrained and completely free. It is learned in reading the poets of the past, in understanding poetry as a way of being, a way of life.

At the end of the world, on the brink of extinction, we have finally begun to understand that language is alive. And that when we use it, we are divining a reality yet unrealized.

Poetry is where I go to become an architect of survival. I am abstracting survival, because I do not and cannot think of survival in concrete terms, because the world we've created and inherited does not want us to survive. Survival for the human being necessitates abstraction, it requires that we see outside the limitations of what is considered real. I use poetry to orient

---

* Aimé Césaire, *In Lyric and Dramatic Poetry 1946–82* (University Press of Virginia, 1990).

myself in the worlds I occupy. How am I situated within the imagination of the oppressor? Does my work make their job easier or harder? Do I puncture the oppressor's fantasies, or am I punctured instead? Moten and Stefano tell us about what it means to puncture: "We preserve upheaval sent to fulfill by abolishing, to renew by unsettling, to open the enclosure whose immeasurable venality is inversely proportionate to its actual area, we got politics surrounded. We cannot represent ourselves. We can't be represented."[*]

We resist the *"enclosure"*—that which encircles us and entraps us within the terms of its perpetual crises—by surrounding *it*, by breaking its gears, by shaking it up with our new and ancient logics.

When we recognize that access to poetry is free and that we all have the opportunity to use it, then we take language's intimacies back, and we take it away from those who abuse it. Language belongs to the hungry, and if we seek nourishment from a future that feeds us all, then language will be the thing that frees us.

I write you a poem that folds in on itself, an epic account, a single stanza as document, itself the first and the last. I write with the hope that we can—and will—choose to construct a language of compassion. Because language is what governs us.

---

[*] Stefano Harney and Fred Moten, *The Undercommons: Fugitive Planning and Black Study* (Autonomedia, 2013).

CHAPTER 1

THE INTRODUCTION

I was born in New York City and raised on the concrete of the Bronx, but every weekend I would sojourn to the Junction Boulevard stop on the 7 train in Queens, where my father's mother lived. Whenever I walked into her house, I could feel her longing for the Grenada that birthed her reflected throughout the small apartment. It was in the colors of the walls, the smells of the food, the sounds of her lilting accent cackling on the phone with a friend from back home. She had left Grenada when my dad was nine to work and send money back to the island, an experience that many Caribbean immigrants know too well. He did not see her again until he was fifteen.

I have a photo of her at a party in Grenada in which she looks like the subject of the room's interest. She is beautiful, and the man next to her seems embarrassed by her beauty, as if he can't believe his luck. She is standing straight, face mostly unsmiling except for a little lift at the corner of her mouth, her purse tucked in the crook of her arm. When I would ask her about Grenada, all she would say was how much she wished she could go back, back to the little island where she felt most beautiful, where the weather agreed with her arthritis, where the parties were good. I try to see the world she inhabited through her eyes. I see her dancing with the cute boy from the mountains, the moonlight setting on her shoulder as she brings her hand up to his chest. After she left the island and became my grandmother, I held that same soft, papery hand in mine on a crowded subway platform.

My grandmother's love was felt through labor—the yellow plantains boiled and rice and peas steaming on the stove when my cousins and I arrived Friday evening at her small, red-carpeted apartment for our weekend stay; the cable subscription she bought just so we could watch Saturday morning cartoons; the money she slipped into our pockets on our way home on Sundays.

Away from her home, thrust into the overwhelm of New York City, we were her greatest achievements. She loved being a grandmother (though, as any Caribbean person would understand, she was a rough-handed grandmother) and took the responsibility of keeping us safe in a world too dangerous and ugly. Even in early childhood, I knew that she was fighting to protect me against something I couldn't see. I saw it when she prayed. I saw it when she brushed her wig and adjusted it just right for the workday. I felt it as she gripped my hand extra tight when we rode the subway. She was afraid for me. And rightly so.

A slow, excruciating kindling of awareness had been tindering beneath my skin for a long time, from early childhood when I first learned that people treated each other differently because of differences neither had a part in deciding upon, like skin color, religion, country of birth. It grew exponentially as I learned about slavery and the systematic dehumanization of Black people all around the world.

It was Trayvon Martin's death that first caused the conflagration. It grounded me in fury. George Zimmerman, a former neighborhood watch captain, took the meaning of his job very seriously. While it is a voluntary role, with no actual legal authority at all, Zimmerman felt himself necessary to the fabric-making of policing. On the other end of that solipsistic self-importance was Trayvon Martin's life. Despair hadn't quite set in, just a feeling of defiance. That defiance that makes you want to run up against a wall to prove that there is nothing up against you. I imagined myself invincible, because that is what defiance does, it armors you with a version of yourself that is willing to say no to death.

At this point, I was a regular at protests, a teacher of Black and Brown kids in Harlem who deserved to be seen by someone who could understand their culture and their language. I wrote what I call political poems, and poems about liberation, and poems about the contradictions of U.S.-defined freedoms. Pissed off and defiant, I pushed myself to evaluate my commitment to activism and Black liberation. Was my poetry enough? Was my job enough? I knew I could not physically stop a bullet from taking my students—did that make me a liar? Impassioned and ready to fight, I became a "good soldier" for justice, one who swore to do more good than harm in every circumstance possible.

Then, only two years later, in August 2014, a police officer killed young Michael Brown in Ferguson, Missouri. That winter I lay in Washington Square Park beside a collection of other bodies lying still on the cold ground. Feet walked around us, over us, in between us, as if we were invisible, as if our bodies were not there. Some people stopped to take pictures, looking around for the yellow tape that would typically close this scene off to bystanders. But there was no tape. Just our bodies on the ground of Washington Square Park, which is, ironically, a park created in the wake of the violent displacement of thousands of Black people who once lived on the land it occupies.

This was my contribution to that era of Black Lives Matter protests: a small initiative that organized die-ins in public places, an action that simulated death so that people who were ignoring our collective cry for justice would feel something visceral when they saw our bodies on the ground. It's a tactic meant to garner empathy, anger, frustration, apathy, and even disgust. I knew that our work as performance artists would be useful to the protest—we could leverage and transform empathy, anger, disgust into other emotions. We could activate people with those emotions.

We were called POC4Solvency, and our core demand, the language we put on our signs, our bodies, and our art, was "We Charge Genocide!"

At one such protest, I lay on the ground with my megaphone to my mouth as I led a chant, which would eventually distill into silence as we all lay there in the cold quiet, our eyes closed, doing death. At one point I opened my eyes to see a handful of white people standing over us, just watching, like an audience at a flash-mob performance. Feeling overexposed and even a bit silly, I thought about the utility of the spectacle. I believed then, and believe now to a certain extent, that spectacular protest had a place in our movement. I wasn't wrong, but I was confused about my goal. Was it to make people who already knew about what was happening become more sympathetic? I began to realize that we had created a spectacle without any strategic direction. I didn't know what our protest was meant to do, I only knew what I wanted people to feel. Once a confident young activist, I became confused. How was change supposed to happen? And would playing dead bring me any closer?

It was Michael Brown's face, his plump cheeks and soft brown eyes, that troubled me most as news of his murder continued to emerge. It was the way he looked into the camera with his simple, reserved smile. It was as if he were seeing something he had seen before, perhaps a haunting from a past life, perhaps a previous life that had ended like this one. I could see everything I had ever known in his eyes—my life, my younger siblings' lives, the life of my then-lover. Life had become a new kind of grief, the grief of confirmation: I knew then, more concretely and more surely than I'd ever known it, that my life and the lives of my diasporic kin, exiles within the metropole, were not safe from time or history. I knew then that Black people in this country were still being hunted, despite the progress our first Black president suggested. It was this realization that made me feel that I needed to get closer to power, I needed to get closer to language to get closer to power. I knew that language could be a weapon, and I wanted to see if I could turn it against the powerful. This was the premise of my experiment.

It wasn't hard to make the connection between what had happened to Trayvon Martin and what had happened to Michael Brown. It was at this realization that Trayvon and Michael were killed by the same white supremacist logic that shaped our world, the logic that said that some of us needed to be controlled and others of us needed to be in control, that the despair turned up, dressed still in defiance, dressed still in rage. It dyed my clothes black, it helped me tuck my hair behind my ears, it geared me up to fight. Who was I fighting? I didn't know.

After Trayvon and Michael, Freddie Gray was murdered by police in Baltimore, and protesters took to the streets. Quickly we learned that representation had a hole in it, where our ideas of justice dematerialized and became more fantasy than policy. We expected President Obama to decry the actions of the racist police and stand unequivocally with protesters, like the second coming of Martin Luther King, Jr. We expected that he'd call off the antagonistic, militarized special forces sent to quell the protest. He didn't. He hedged and stood tall in two-sides-ism, referring to angry protesters as thugs and calling the uprising a distraction and counterproductive to the more "peaceful" protesters who were doing it "the right way." As all kinds of protesters were being teargassed and military tanks bouldered through Black metros terrorizing communities, the president took the side of everyone and no one.

"I think there are police departments that have to do some soul-searching. I think there are some communities that have to do some soul-searching," President Obama said. "But I think we, as a country have to do some soul-searching."

What we expected of then–President Obama was beyond what the framework of the presidency allowed. We expected a panacea. When he was on the campaign trail and was running for president, there was still a part of him that was ours: the organizer from Chicago. We knew that he had cut his teeth on the stones of our history. But the day he became president of the United States, he became the figurehead of the ruling class, a symbol of its evolution toward a new racial permeability that would create a new, racially integrated class of leaders that would ultimately continue to serve the project of neoliberalism and its genesis, white supremacy. That was a heartbreaking realization. Some of us came to it sooner than others.

But it would be reductive of me to say that representation and representation politics have given us nothing. I loved the dream of the First Black President, and I cherished President Obama. I was moved by the poetics of what representation could mean, moved by the endless metaphors it offered up about Blackness's survivability and resistance. But what I discovered is that representation is, fundamentally, a metaphor. We say *There is power in representation,* because power is the thing we want to know more about. And when we talk about representation in our politics, what we're trying to understand is how power works, and then how to emulate it. This is representation's true utility: It tells us what we need to know about power so that we can get around it. It's not the nail, it's the hammer.

What I began to understand about power on the day of Obama's remarks on the Baltimore uprising was that the power of the people might never translate to the presidency. It started to dawn on me, this complex knowing that would reshape my entire political identity—that emulating the power structures that govern us could only get us so far. When representation is weaponized without a radical politics, it is never enough.

In 2015 my activism had made me visible, which made me attractive to a nonprofit named DoSomething.org, an organization meant to activate young people and move them toward activism and voting. Obama's remarks on Freddie Gray enraged me, which was disorienting and offensive to the white liberal CEO and COO who had hired me. As the person tasked with watching the news and telling the rest of the organization what was happening in real time, I felt it was my job to try to articulate to my colleagues just how violent and harmful his hedging was. I was given a stern talking-to after using some not-so-nice language to describe the president's actions and realized then that my perspective on how activism should work was incongruent with what white liberals thought change looked like. They were so satisfied with the idea of a Black president that there was no room for valid critical analysis. I was thought to be problematic, a liability for the organization. Soon, leadership became hostile, a mirror of how liberals maintain hostility toward radical change, and I knew it was time to go. On recommendation from the chair, I applied to the Arts Politics program at NYU and got in, for the second time, to a graduate program without first having earned a bachelor's degree. I asked my boss, the now disgraced CEO Nancy Lublin,* if I could do this program and continue to work at DoSomething.org. Though another employee (a white woman who was a favorite of the CEO) had been ap-

---

* In 2020, Nancy Lublin would be removed as CEO from her organization Crisis Text Line after former Crisis Text Line and DoSomething employees launched a campaign in protest against years of racist and hostile workplace practices.

proved to study at the same university and work for the org at the same time, Nancy said no. She then told me that she could get me into a bachelor's program at the New School if I wanted to go back to school. This was an attempt at belittling me, as she had become even more condescending and dismissive toward me since the Obama debacle.

At a retreat, just weeks after getting into NYU, I was fired for speaking up about the way we were treating Black activists during the Black Lives Matter protests—collecting them for our own visibility but offering no substantive support. Nancy asked me to step out into the hallway, where she berated me for having the audacity to challenge her. "I believed in you, I'm the only person who believed in you," she said, so angry that her face had turned tomato red. "But I don't anymore."

She called me a car and told me that she would mail me my things. I walked out of that conference space with my dignity injured after suffering those ten minutes (and one year) of psychological torture, but with the understanding that the universe had sent me a sign—no nonprofit with a Disney personality would be able to help make meaningful change during a moment of heightened violence against Black activists.

This outcome was a clear sign that my interests were not just cultural but political, and I knew that I needed to chase that thread of thought to move closer to the questions that mattered. The questions I wanted answers to (Is there a world where Black people are safe from subjugation and oppression? If so, is that a world we vote for or a world we struggle for? Is voting a radical act or a compulsive act? Can the same apparatus that enslaved us be the thing that frees us?) couldn't be explored from a desk inside an office designed for millennial workers—beanbags, meditation rooms, you know, the works. That was too easy.

Once I entered the program at NYU, my mind opened up in a way it could not have before. I began to study Black liberation movements—paying close attention to the Black Panther Party, to MOVE activists, to thinkers like Kwame Ture and Elaine Brown and Maurice Bishop and Ruth Wilson Gilmore and Angela Davis and Assata Shakur and Dionne Brand and Christina Sharpe, Sylvia Wynter and George Jackson, and . . . I began a long, sometimes confusing, endless study of Marx and Lenin in an effort to better understand the frameworks of the liberation ideologies and systems of solidarity that they were working from. I went to them with the intent to glean a sense of what it meant to be a colonized people, what it meant to be a "citizen," what it meant to belong within a geography, what it meant to be a human being, what it meant to be a Black human being, what it meant to be stateless, what it meant to live within a democracy, what it meant to submit to democracy, how democracy's mechanics really worked, what revolution meant, what peace meant. Was it chicken or egg? Does social change beget legislative change or vice versa? I wanted to know how true social change was designed and executed. I needed to know it was possible.

Sylvia taught me that the very idea of humanness must be deconstructed to decenter the "genres" of humanness—whiteness, wealth, heteroness, maleness, ableness—that qualify the humanness of some while they disqualify those of us on the margins as nonhuman, thus redefining what it means to be a

Black human being altogether. Ture taught me that Black people's relationship to Blackness must change, and that in that change is a recognition that we have been used to produce the world and are victims of a nation-state that requires the exploitation of the enslaved in order to thrive.

Ruth Wilson Gilmore taught me that racial capitalism is the battery that powers the nation's back.

Marx taught me that the nation-state is inherently capitalist, and that capitalism necessarily turns the state into a war machine that capitalizes on conflict in order to survive. Marx also taught me that revolution is inevitable because the working class will eventually rise up against the owner class and exhaust capitalism, thus exhausting the war machine and the conditions that create it.

Angela Davis and Maurice Bishop taught me that revolution is not just attractive but possible. Assata Shakur taught me that freedom is expensive.

Christina Sharpe taught me that to live in the wake is to encounter the past.

In Audre Lorde's famed 1977 essay "Poetry Is Not a Luxury," she declares that poetry is a revolutionary act.* Her choice to call it an act—not an occupation or a belonging but a verb that requires the writer and the reader to *do*—is of important note. Poetry is, following the logic of Lorde, a system of choices that helps us qualify and comprehend our many subjectivities, that helps us identify the nature of oppressive structures, that helps us liberate and defend. Poetry is, Lorde says, "the skeleton architecture of our lives," a framework that leads us toward the

---

* Audre Lorde, *Sister Outsider: Essays and Speeches* (Crossing Press, 1984).

bridge of our fears, on the other side of which exists a world that "has never been before." For Lorde, poetry is not simply a rhetorical tool but a gesture that has the power to illuminate human connectivity and inspire the practice of imagination. In a fractured society, Lorde saw poetry as a microscope that has the power to expose our various interstices. Poetry can call us to action while holding us accountable to truth.

My teacher, the poet Lyrae Van Clief-Stefanon, once said to me, "Stop acting like you don't know what you know," because for a long time (and sometimes still) I did not trust myself. I did not trust that what I'd always known could be true. There were always people who'd read more than me, seen more than me, been exposed to more than me, and ultimately knew something that I could not. I was afraid of being naïve, of knowing the problem but having no answers.

I went to the mentors of our liberation movements because I was looking for answers. Those answers took me to my father's history, my grandmother's history, where I found even more questions. I would soon learn that poetry had the capacity to hold all my questions and their answers.

CHAPTER 2

THE LULLABY AND THE NURSERY RHYME

The first poetic texts offered to many of us are the lullaby and the nursery rhyme. They are our first examples of how a poem can work, both physically and emotionally.

The nursery rhyme introduces poetry to the baby who has turned into a child—lullabies, however, are poems sung to babies to help soothe them, to teach them it is safe to surrender to sleep. But they are also warnings, omens, guides, memories sung in mournful chords. They are often harrowing accounts of ongoing or imminent violence.

One of the lullabies my mother sang to me is called "All the Pretty Little Horses"—an old African American lullaby, written sometime before the Civil War, created first and known most intimately by southern slaves, their descendants, and the children they sang to.*

I was a dramatic child who feared abandonment even early in life, before I knew what it really meant. I remember a night at age four or five when my mother and grandmother tried to put me to bed so that they could watch British detective shows on PBS. I hollered as my mother tucked me into the bed we shared, screaming "I'm having a heart attack" as she tried to soothe me with her lush, smooth voice that I could hear over my cries. I fell asleep to the scent of frankincense, my hands tangled in her dreadlocks, and the lullaby never stopped playing in my head:

> Go to sleepy, little baby.
> When you wake,
> You shall have cake,
> All the pretty little horses.
> Blacks and bays
> Dapples and grays,
> Coach and six a little horses.
> Hush-a-bye,
> Don't you cry,
> Go to sleep, my little baby.

There are many iterations of this song, and many interpretations. One reading suggests that it is being sung to the child of a slave master by the Black mammy figure who bears the bur-

---

* Dorothy Scarborough, *On the Trail of Negro Folk-Songs* (Harvard University Press, 1925).

den of comforting a child who is stealing time away from her own baby. I imagine the singer laying her own child on the ground of her shelter. She watches her hungry baby sleep, led gently to its death, led into its infinity, because she has no milk to feed them, because her milk has been taken by the children of the master, the children she is forced to care for at the expense of the health and wellness of her own children. The poem reveals a woman coming face-to-face with her powerlessness.

> Hush-a-bye,
> Don't you cry,
> Go to sleepy, little baby.
> Way down yonder
> In de medder
> There's a po' lil lambie,
> De bees an' de butterflies
> Peckin' out its eyes
> De po' lil thing cried "Mammy!"
> Hush-a-bye,
> Don't you cry
> Go to sleep, my little baby.*

The singer's coo in "Pretty Little Horses" is both relief and rage. She is hoping that on the other end of her baby's torture is a heaven of riches. And if she sang this to the child she'd been forced to care for after her own child died, the coo is both re-

---

* John A. Lomax and Alan Lomax, *American Ballads and Folk Songs* (Macmillan, 1934), Internet Archive, archive.org/details/americanballadsf00loma.

sentful and, rightfully, hateful. She knows that the child will wake to its inherited riches, while her child will never wake again.

Today, the song is sung as a song of comfort, a song of will. And it does exactly what the singer aims. It puts their baby to sleep with the promise of beauty. But it also reproduces the anxiety that was born from subjugation. Even without intent, we reproduce the language that is meant to kill us.

>   Eenie Meenie Miney Mo
>   Catch a fella by his toe
>   If he hollers, let him go
>   Eenie Meenie Miney Mo.

I have a distinct memory of my mother singing "Eenie Meenie Miney Mo" to me, pulling each of my toes as she sang each word of the song. And when she got to the end of the song, she would pretend to bite off the toe she'd selected.

In middle school, I sang "Eenie Meenie Miney Mo" as I picked my team for kickball, pointing with each word at a kid waiting to be selected, ending at that last syllable with a finger directed at the kid of my choice. I remember the student running toward me after being chosen, as if running away from the rest of the group.

That nursery rhyme showed up throughout my childhood: "Eenie Meenie Miney Mo" has been ingrained in our various Western cultures, a staple of the parent's toolbox of play, meant to engage and stimulate their children. Versions can be traced back to Denmark, France, Zimbabwe. The lullaby, or poem, is not an inherently vicious song created to terrorize Black children—its syllabic patterns and its "trochaic and dactylic"* meter can be found in songs of different languages, sung all over the world—but this American version is a threat.

The speaker is addressing the enslaved, reminding them of what might happen if they attempt to escape. This stanza is even more explicit:

> Eenie meenie miney mo,
> Catch a nigger by his toe;
> Every time the nigger hollers,
> make him pay you fifty dollars.†

The song was a reminder to the negro that his freedom doesn't exist, that any attempt at freedom will be met by its limitation, that any attempt at freedom will cost him his labor and cost him his life. The language of this nursery rhyme makes clear the violence the colonizer uses to describe the enslaved's destiny. And then the nursery rhyme begins again at its end, "If he hollers, let him go / Eenie Meenie ... ," promising us a return to the beginning of the poem, where recapture and reenslavement are already guaranteed. The poem is essentially a pantoum—a poetic form of four-line stanzas in which the last line mirrors the first—a form that intentionally suggests cyclicality, a poem that never ends, a limit that doesn't exist.

During gym, when we sang that song to pick teams for kickball, we knew nothing about its context. Even now, the

---

* Henry Carrington Bolton, *The Counting-Out Rhymes of Children: Their Antiquity, Origin, and Wide Distribution; a Study in Folk-Lore* (E. Stock, 1888).

† Bolton, *Counting-Out Rhymes*.

pantoum lives in my head, and it feels dirty, like an intrusive thought. Nearly all of the students in my class were Black and Brown children born from the legacies of slavery. In the frigid dark of the winter months after kickball at afterschool, I walked to the bus that would take me home. Across the street from the bus stop was a juvenile jail. I had to watch my friends enter and disappear and then return home only to reenter. I had no words then to describe what it felt like in my belly whenever I walked past that juvenile hall, its lone basketball hoop obscured behind a wall of barbed wire. But now I know that I was feeling the incalculable weight of perpetuity. The seeds of those seemingly innocuous lullabies and nursery rhymes, which were planted long before my birth, first in the legal documents that shaped the world I was born into, drafted by the same people who sang those songs, and their progeniture. Those seeds became how I first viewed myself, my future, my community. Until I bored down and pulled the roots.

In 2011, I took a Black Studies course at Hostos Community College. My professor was a tenured Black Studies and Egyptology scholar who embodied the aesthetics of his scholarship: the kente cloth, the ankh painted on the wall of his office. He could command a classroom like nobody's business, enticing his students with endless analysis of how our society's foundational makeup has been shaped by anti-Blackness and lectures on Black exceptionalism. I remain skeptical of a lot of it, skeptical of any kind of eugenicist logic that made Black people inherently exceptional or inherently enslaved, really anything that suggests we were other than human, but it stirred something in me, triggered a consciousness that would soon lead to an interest in understanding the political moment we were living in and its historical context.

At the same time, I was taking courses on student activism and civics that assigned us Howard Zinn's *A People's History of the United States* and the Constitution, which gave me a framework for understanding the poems of my childhood and historical documents in a new light, helping me to think about complicity and collusion in a way I hadn't before. I was already deep into my poetry practice, but I was still learning, of course, about the power of illusion and narrative and the poetics of the political, so when our Black Studies professor introduced us to the papal bull *Romanus Pontifex* of 1455, I was unprepared for its profundity.

In the fourteenth century, the Portuguese had arrived in West African territories and made note of the people's intelligence and their capacity for world-building labor that sustained their communities. The Portuguese returned from their travels and moved quickly to consecrate ownership over these territories and their people, eager to visit upon them the worst evils of colonial force. The legalization of this intent came from the Catholic Church, which was considered the mouthpiece of God. In 1452, Pope Nicholas V, in collaboration with King Afonso V of Portugal, released a papal bull called *Dum Diversas*—which is not a doctrine but a statement from the Vatican that decreed that all Muslims, pagans, and nonbelievers in Christ be enslaved by the king. Later that year, Pope Nicholas V issued a mandate to King Afonso that took this bull even further, addressing to him an instruction, written as God's word, to go about this duty with whatever force and strategy were needed to honor the decree and subdue all non-Christians into ownership:

> to reduce their persons into perpetual slavery, and to apply and appropriate and convert to the use and profit of yourself and your successors, the Kings of Portugal, in perpetuity.*

In 1454, he reproduced this language in a longer brief to King Afonso V, and after a series of revisions, he reproduced the language *again* in the renewal of this permission in the papal bull *Romanus Pontifex* of 1455. Issued on behalf of the Roman Empire, this was not a legal document but a letter encouraging the thinking that would formalize Portugal's monopoly of trade in the West African region, closing the region off from the rest of the world, effectively lassoing it into compliance through force, sanctioning the enslavement of even more African people and initiating the Atlantic slave trade.

The papal bull of 1455 took *Dum Diversas* a step forward, making this permission legal, no longer a suggestion, granting the Portuguese full monopoly over non-Christian lands and expanding and facilitating the Portuguese slave trade throughout West Africa.

These iterations of the original *Dum Diversas* make up the flesh of the Doctrine of Discovery, a poem of nefarious ambition. The pope and the king were excellent poets, thought makers who imagined a world in which every person on earth was a subject and manifested it through the crafting of each docu-

---

* Nicholas V, *Romanus Pontifex* (1455).

ment, reproduced again and again by what preceded it, reinforced throughout history; taken together, the documents insist on themselves and write themselves into fruition. These documents have different cosmetic qualities but are all actually the same. They all insist on inhumanity, insist on white supremacy, and rely on poetry to articulate that insistence:

> . . . to invade, search out, capture, vanquish, and subdue all Saracens and pagans whatsoever, and other enemies of Christ wheresoever placed, and the kingdoms, dukedoms, principalities, dominions, possessions, and all movable and immovable goods whatsoever held and possessed by them and to reduce their persons to perpetual slavery, and to apply and appropriate to himself and his successors the kingdoms, dukedoms, counties, principalities, dominions, possessions, and goods, and to convert them to his and their use and profit—by having secured the said faculty, the said King Afonso, or, by his authority, the aforesaid infante, justly and lawfully has acquired and possessed, and doth possess, these islands, lands, harbors, and seas, and they do of right belong and pertain to the said King Afonso and his successors . . .

These fifteenth-century papal edicts were not just expressions of fantastic desire, but strategic declarations meant to do exactly what they set out to do: extort, enslave, dominate, and expatriate all non-white / non-Anglo / non-Christian peoples—armed with God's glory and God's armies.

If the pope and the king were poets of the worst world, then the language of their rule was meant to subdue and repress, a lullaby sung to the ruling class and the poor alike. It was a promise that Christ had endorsed, to grant these riches, this wealth, to his followers.

It said that there was a world of riches on the other side of the ocean, a world they could all live in. That vision put Europe to sleep with its promise, with its comfort, while its flagitious implications obscured the second meaning of the edict: the silencing of anyone not of the elite.

This papal bull of 1455 helped to set the terms of engagement, a document that takes its time and an economy of language to spell out the involute and complete ways in which the Christian Church would become the Father and hold divine dominance over the entire globe, in the name of Christ.

Soon after my learning about the papal bulls of 1452 and 1455 came an understanding that these documents did not function on their own. I learned that they were just part of the grand tapestry of domination that the colonizing powers envisioned.

The document that followed, the document that charts the beginning of the end of the world, is a bull called the Doctrine of Discovery, a bull that grants permission to the aspirational young men of royal blood to do what they please, to dominate every part of the world that sees the sun, in service of the empire of Christ. The beginning of the end of the world builds on the series of papal bulls, including those of 1452 and 1455, that sanctioned the destruction of our physical and spiritual worlds, each of which documents the progeniture of the one that came before. The language of the law is a dark lullaby that steals from the poetics of God to lull us into quiet, lull us to sleep.

It is in these critical moments, when the lullaby pulls us into stopped-time, that the devil gets in. And the devil is no person or figure, of no religion or creed—the devil is the transfer of evil from thought into action. Heaven became hell the moment when the young aspirational man was granted the empire in return for his service to Christ and took the empire to do what he pleased, not what pleases Christ (as he said he was channeling) or the people of empire. The devil is a man who decides to play God, doing what he wants with bodies that do not belong to him.

When my mother sang "All the Pretty Little Horses" to us, she felt the urgency of my life. She sang this song because she wanted to protect me from my own cries, because she wanted peace for both of us. She sang it to put me to sleep, to soothe the ancestors still mourning through me. The song recognizes history, and every terror that comes with it, and even if it didn't come to her consciously, she sang with the intuitive knowing that the song acknowledged: that she might never see me wake.

Once enslaved people had been brought to the Americas, Europeans began to write laws to dictate how the lives of the people they kidnapped should be governed. This legal framework that codified slavery and affirmed the social order in which slaves were deemed nonhuman in the Americas, and most critically in the Caribbean, should be understood as the natural progression of those fifteenth-century documents that codified chattel slavery and the Atlantic slave trade, building on and extending the scale of the documents' aims.

In 1690, South Carolina's earliest slave code, the first slave code enacted in the British colonies, was established, setting off an infectious proliferation of slave codes throughout the mainland colonies. These codes formalized slave owners' absolute right to inflict violence or death on the enslaved at their whim and discretion. They made the slitting of a slave's nose or a burn on the face permissible as a strategy for "The Better Ordering of Slaves." South Carolina's slave code did not arrive from the imagination of the colony's order. South Carolina's slave code came forth through the formation of Barbados's slave code, enshrined into law in 1661. South Carolina's slave code echoed the Bajan slave code in its proposed justification, with some clauses even pulled directly from the original document. In the establishment of the South Carolina slave codes, the Caribbean islands and the plantations of the southern North American continent gained another material history, and its influence spread throughout the Caribbean and seventeenth-century America.

Slave codes—these laws titled by their intention to dominate the enslaved and to assert the absence of freedom on the part of the enslaved—evolved into the systems of policing that came to be in Britain, the U.S., and the Caribbean colonies. Policing is the progeniture of all the slave codes that came before it.

> And whereas the Inhabitants of this Island have much suffred by the runing away of their Negroes and by the injurious keeping of such Runaway or Fugitive Negroes by severall persons in their Plantations It is hereby Enacted published and declared by the authority aforesaid that all persons who are now possessed of any Fugitive or Runaway Negroes do within six dayes after the publication of this Act

in the Parish Churches bring them in and deliver them to the proper Owners or into the Custody of the Provost Marshall for the time being or his appointed Deputy at the Towne of St. Michaels upon paine of paying Ten Thousand pounds as good Merchantable Muscovado Sugar for damage unto the Owner . . .*

As the need to police slaves grew, slave codes in the post-revolutionary U.S. evolved; slave patrol, the act of enforcing the policing of slaves within the jurisdiction of the slave codes, is policing's vehicle, the thing that makes the terror tangible. Slave patrols were designed to surveil the enslaved and punish them for perceived transgressions that called for the exacting power of the patrol. The South Carolina 1690 slave code specified,

And it is further Enacted by the authority aforesaid that noe person whatsoever except the Sheriff or Gaoler shall keepe any runaway Slave or Slaves above four dayes.†

"Eenie Meenie Miney Mo" is a poetic instruction, a note to the enslaved and the owner class: The slave is akin to any animal, a nonhuman meant to be captured, released, then captured again in the cycle of its own enslavement. It also suggests that any member of the ruling class can apprehend an enslaved person, making them arbiters of abstract justice who believe they

---

* Barbados Slave Codes of 1661, *Slavery Law & Power in Early America and the British Empire* (slaverylawpower.org).

† 1690 Carolina Slave Code, *Slavery Law & Power in Early America and the British Empire* (slaverylawpower.org).

are sharing the duties of maintaining order within their communities. They catch, they release, and they catch again in a sick game of cyclical power. The code also serves to ensure that any person who houses a runaway slave is penalized for their complicity. Still, in this dynamic lies the conceit of ownership: that the slave belongs to its owner, and thus no one but the owner should be able to keep a slave in their custody.

> Eenie Meenie Miney Mo
> Catch a fella by his toe
> If he hollers, let him go . . .

The language of these lullabies and nursery rhymes is evidence of the reproduction and enforcement of ideas centered on dominating Black bodies, the same ideas that have been effectively woven into society's fabrics. This is how efficiently language becomes a weapon. The South Carolina Slave Code of 1740, no. 670, proclaims:

> . . . all Negroes and Indians, (free Indians in amity with this government, and degrees, mulattoes, and mustizoes, who are now free, excepted,) mulattoes or mustizoes who now are, or shall hereafter be, in this Province, and all their issue and offspring, born or to be born, shall be, and they are hereby declared to be, and remain forever hereafter, absolute slaves, and shall follow the condition of the mother . . .

The South, like the Caribbean, is made heavy by its legacies of slavery. Colonial Georgia and colonial South Carolina crafted and enforced some of the most severe slave laws in the colonial United States. Those laws were revived and made more severe after Georgia was granted statehood, and the necessity of stronger slave laws necessitated modes of enforcement. A 1770 slave law required every slave owner who kept ten or more slaves over the age of sixteen to also keep a white man capable of bearing arms as an overseer, manager, or superintendent. A 1765 slave law concerning patrols required that all white men between the age of sixteen and sixty must participate in slave patrols, must examine all plantations in their district once every fourteen days, and must punish a slave by whipping. The same law required that those on patrol carry a gun or pistol and ammunition while on patrol, and gave those on patrol the power to search "slave houses" for weapons. That's what it means to "catch a tiger by the toe." In 1817, the state penitentiary was established, turning these same local patrol leaders into local police captains and officers. Slave patrols continued to operate in Georgia until slavery was abolished following the Civil War. Policing in the state of Georgia and all throughout the South (particularly in the colonial Carolinas) evolved when slavery laws died and Black Codes—laws established after the Civil War to restrain Black freedom—were born. This song plays in the background as our children run through the playground.

But what emboldens me is the thought that new poems are written in its place, poems steeped in the language of liberation, care, and freedom that our children of today may memorize.

The state clings to its legacies of slavery, even as it purports to seek distance from those legacies, because it has no alternate material. Because the dragon cannot slay itself.

—

Marcellus "Khaliifah" Williams, who was executed by the state of Missouri in 2024, was a radical poet who spent his twenty-four years on death row embodying the practice of solidarity through his work. He wrote poems for fellow prisoners on death row, for people on the outside whose despair he could understand, to himself for comfort. Before he was killed, in one of his final revolutionary acts, he penned a poem for Palestine. Mournful and demanding, this poem exemplifies the wholeness and circularity of abolitionist logic. Marcellus knew that the occupation is as much a prison as the walls that held him; therefore, he understood that every Palestinian is a political prisoner. Marcellus knew that an escape from occupation is an escape from the plantation, and that an escape from the plantation is a prison break.

Despite the insistence of the language of history, the language of freedom rings through. Marcellus, even under the constraints of incarceration, saw poetry's ability to access a kind of freedom. Marcellus, giving voice to the millions of other Black people who suffer the modern enslavement of incarceration, actively subverts the language of history while crafting new language, new lullabies, that point at what the future should be, as in his poem "The Perplexing Smiles of the Children of Palestine":[*]

> despite the actions of the few
> And excessive retaliation,

---

[*] Marcellus "Khaliifah" Williams, "The Perplexing Smiles of the Children of Palestine," *Tempest Collective,* October 2, 2024.

drones,
planes,
bombs,
tanks,
rubble,
buildings demolished,
vanished houses and neighborhoods,
hospitals targeted,
U.N. shelters disrespected,
murder,
death,
deliberate killing of noncombatants,
babies buried alive,
amputations,
hunger and political starvation,
lack of or no water,
strategic sanitation,
daily terror,
and terrorized daily,
military maneuvering,
moving here and there,
to return back again to nowhere,
trauma with all its manifestations,
international prayers and hesitation,
defiance to the realization of two nations,
global aid thwarted,
global amnesia,
siblings and relatives gone forever,
parental worries —
in the face of apex arrogance

> and ethnic cleansing by any definition . . .
> still your laughter can be heard
> and somehow you are able to smile,
> O resilient Children of Palestine!

Every line, every mark, represents a dialogue; the mind defying the prison, defying the lullabies of history that restrict him to a life of enslavement that his ancestors knew first. Where incarcerated people are without citizenship and without dignity is where solidarity, rebellion, and the radical germinate. And they are impossible to quell.

The spirit of rebellion, born from the hearts of the enslaved on plantations in the U.S. and in the Caribbean, lives in the bodies of the incarcerated who inevitably come to know of their status within the cycle of repression and freedom. The prison is a container in which radicalization thrives. The effect of slave codes on history, the present, and the future is like the nursery rhyme; it is cyclical, coming back in different material but saying the same thing over and over again.

Mothers still sing hush-a-bye; children still sing "Eenie Meenie"—a sign of the insidiousness of the language of the state that has punctured history, has traveled through centuries, and has been reproduced over and over to uphold the wishes of the conqueror. In this song, sung from a child's mouth, is the reification of the intent of the code laws: "to capture, and capture again."

Freedom is a pantoum. The language of the oppressor is alive. But so is the language of the oppressed.

Excerpts from the South Carolina Slave Code (1740)

Note: The erased text has been cut down for readability.

WHEREAS ▮ His Majesty ▮▮▮▮
▮▮▮▮▮▮▮▮▮▮▮▮▮▮▮▮
▮▮▮▮▮▮▮▮▮▮▮▮▮▮▮▮
▮▮▮▮▮▮▮▮▮▮▮▮▮▮▮▮
▮▮▮▮▮▮▮▮▮▮▮▮▮▮▮▮
▮▮▮▮▮▮▮▮▮▮▮▮▮▮▮▮
▮▮ may disturb
the ▮▮▮▮▮▮▮▮▮▮▮▮
▮▮▮▮▮▮▮▮▮▮▮▮▮▮▮▮
▮▮▮▮▮▮▮▮▮▮▮▮▮▮▮▮
▮▮▮▮

▮▮▮▮▮▮▮▮▮▮▮▮▮▮▮▮
▮ free Negro,
▮▮▮▮▮▮▮▮▮▮▮▮▮▮▮▮
▮▮▮▮▮▮▮▮▮▮▮▮▮▮▮▮
▮▮▮▮ insurrection ▮▮▮▮
▮▮▮▮▮
▮▮▮▮▮▮
▮▮▮▮▮▮▮▮▮▮▮▮▮▮▮▮
▮▮▮

  may

alter the sentence

4

LET THE POETS GOVERN - 41

▆▆▆▆▆▆▆▆▆▆▆▆▆▆▆▆▆▆▆▆▆▆▆▆
▆▆ And for that ▆ it is absolutely necessary ▆▆▆▆
▆▆ that ▆
▆▆▆▆▆▆▆▆▆▆▆▆ the wanderings and meetings of
Negroes ▆▆▆▆▆▆
▆▆▆▆▆▆▆▆▆▆▆▆▆▆▆▆▆▆▆▆▆▆▆▆
▆▆▆
▆▆▆▆▆▆▆▆▆▆▆▆▆▆▆▆▆▆▆▆▆▆▆▆
▆
▆▆▆▆▆▆▆▆▆▆▆▆▆▆▆▆▆▆▆▆▆▆▆▆
▆▆▆
▆▆▆▆▆▆▆▆▆▆▆▆▆▆▆▆▆ be ▆▆ diligently
▆▆
▆▆▆▆▆▆▆▆▆▆▆▆▆▆▆▆▆▆▆▆▆▆▆▆
▆
▆▆▆▆▆▆▆▆▆▆▆▆▆▆▆▆▆▆▆▆▆▆▆▆
▆▆
▆▆▆▆▆ offensive ▆▆▆▆▆▆
▆▆▆▆▆▆▆▆▆▆▆▆▆▆▆▆▆▆▆▆▆▆▆▆
▆▆
▆▆▆▆▆▆▆▆▆▆▆▆▆▆▆▆▆▆ beat drums,
blow horns, ▆ use
▆▆▆▆▆▆▆▆▆▆▆▆▆▆▆▆▆▆▆▆▆▆▆▆
▆
▆▆▆▆▆▆▆▆▆▆▆▆▆▆▆▆

▆▆▆▆▆▆▆▆▆▆▆▆▆▆▆▆▆▆▆▆▆▆▆▆
▆▆
▆ humanity ▆▆▆ to restrain ▆▆▆ barbarity ▆▆

▄▄▄▄

▄▄▄▄▄▄▄▄▄▄▄▄▄▄▄▄

▄▄▄▄

▄▄▄▄▄▄▄▄▄▄▄▄▄▄▄▄

▄▄▄▄▄

▄▄▄▄

▄ And whereas ▄▄▄▄▄▄▄▄ suffering

▄▄▄

▄▄▄▄▄ may be attended with great inconveniences ▄

▄▄▄

▄▄▄▄▄▄▄▄▄▄▄▄▄▄▄▄

▄▄▄▄

▄▄▄▄▄▄▄▄▄▄

▄▄▄▄▄▄▄▄▄▄▄▄▄▄▄▄

▄▄

▄▄▄▄▄▄ no person ▄▄▄▄ shall ▄

▄▄▄

▄▄▄ forfeit ▄▄▄▄▄▄

▄▄▄

▄▄

▄▄▄▄

CHAPTER 3

THE PLEDGE

Fugitivity, then, is a desire for and a spirit of escape and transgression of the proper and the proposed. It's a desire for the outside, for a playing or being outside, an outlaw edge proper to the now always already improper voice or instrument.

—Fred Moten

At 8:15 on a morning in September 2004, I exited the 4 train at Mosholu Parkway, my breath making clouds in the dewy air. I steadied myself as students poured from every direction—hundreds descending the staircases of the elevated train station, stumbling from the back doors of buses, rushing toward the big concrete building, like fire ants on their way to the queen. I knew intuitively that there were too many of us.

I followed the crowd until it bottlenecked four city blocks from the entrance to the school, already sweating under the high morning sun. I had no idea what we were waiting for. I stood there, wanting to be noticed but afraid to be seen, envious of the familiarity between the other kids, wondering how they all knew each other and what they would think if they knew me. And in the heat, in the chatter of voices ringing around my head, I was so disoriented that I forgot about time—when I looked down at my watch, it was 9:45. Homeroom started at 9:15. Minutes dotted by like sparks of blue flames in a fire. Though I'd woken up on time and gotten there extra early, I was late on my first day.

Finally I saw the steps to the front entrance, and the DEWITT CLINTON HIGH SCHOOL sign. The line moved with the cadence of "Pomp and Circumstance"—*One student enters, then stop. Another student enters, then stop.* Impatience and anxiety made me indignant, and it took everything in me not to step to the front and ask what the holdup was about.

As I waited, I could see another crowd of kids my age, majority white and Asian, headed down the street toward the entrance of the Bronx High School of Science, just a few blocks away, separated by a gate and some trees, where there was no line. It was their first day of school too, but the students at Bronx Science seemed to float into the entrance without any kind of congestion. A specialized high school for NYC's "most promising," Bronx Science looked so similar to mine—another big concrete building with a football field—that from afar, you could mistake one for the other. But there were no bars on their windows. As soon as I entered my school building, I was told to take off my shoes, belt, and jacket, brusquely frisked, and sent to homeroom. When I walked into my classroom, still adjusting my clothes, the first thing I noticed was that half of my classmates were sitting on the floor because of a lack of seating and an overwhelming number of students per class. I took a seat on the radiator just underneath the barred window. We were allowed to stand only when it was time to recite the Pledge of Allegiance.

"I pledge allegiance to the flag of the United States of America and to the Republic for which it stands, one Nation under God, indivisible, with liberty and justice for all." Since kindergarten, I had been required to make this pledge, which has settled itself well into my brain.

The pledge obligates children into a performative demonstration of patriotism—a full-out assault on their agency—and coerces them into the perpetuation of a narcissistic show of allegiance. What is allegiance anyway? What is liberty? It's an ironic conjecture rooted in militarism and imperialism. Can the flag protect? The threshold to protection is outfitted in the seedy requirements and contradictions of capitalism, where no person can live a free life while earning basic minimum wage. This country has no clue; it kills its subjects for selling cigarettes and sells them opioids, pain management, and addiction. What is allegiance when the entity demanding loyalty violates the freedoms of everything it encloses?

And so, on that first day of high school, as forty students sat like sardines in a schoolroom with guarded, unopened windows and limited seating, I decided not to pledge allegiance. Who was this teacher, or anyone, to require my allegiance to a flag that didn't even guarantee me a seat? By resisting an intellectual falsity, by accepting the invitation to refute the consequence, I was disrupting the expectation that was placed on me—the expectation that I embrace the authority's wrongness and accept my own inferiority.

The American education system is the first place where the imagination of the oppressor is made material in the life of the subordinate. It is presented to us as nonthreatening guidance, even as it willfully makes itself known through the violent imposition of order. We are told to stand in line and be counted, to sit when told, to stand when told, to Simon-says our responses—all manifestations of the authoritarian fantasy the settler state thrives on. We are taught to react when provoked; we are impelled into delusion.

In January 2002, only a few years before I entered high school, No Child Left Behind became the organizing principle for K–12 education in the United States. Signed into law by President George W. Bush, the legislation mandated new testing and "proficiency for all," which it did not succeed at accomplishing. Instead, it forced states to identify schools that were failing to achieve satisfactory scores on standardized tests, and then it set a series of mandates that told states how to "fix" those schools. This created the conditions for a huge exodus of teachers and students from culturally and academically rich schools. State curriculum was shaped by data, completely undermining the function of education—which is to individualize study to each student so that their education is bespoke. NCLB promised nationwide educational equity, but it produced the opposite.* Students of color living below the poverty line were not given the resources to achieve under the standards of NCLB.

Low performance wasn't the difference between the success of minority and non-minority students—systemic racism was. The authors of this law were of course uninterested in this history.

---

* George Wood, "A View from the Field," in *Many Children Left Behind: How the No Child Left Behind Act Is Damaging Our Children and Our Schools* ed. Deborah Meier and George Wood (Beacon Press, 2004).

This dynamic is what led to students, uncomfortably enclosed within the classroom, trained to recite the words of the Pledge of Allegiance dutifully, trying to learn as police officers casually roamed the hallways. Children were criminalized for having the audacity to exist under such duress, left languid without food when the cafeteria ran out, made suspicious of one another by metal detectors. Our teachers told us to tolerate these conditions because we were being "educated," and this was supposed to be our primary liberator; the logic follows that as long as we were receiving an education, this critical limb of the American Dream, we would ultimately have nothing to worry about and should feel grateful, despite the awful quality of this critical limb, despite the limb's failure.

The institution is good at defending itself. When we complained, we were reminded of children in "parts of Africa" who had "no schools" and "no opportunity," and who would, apparently, do anything for our moldy bread at breakfast, our spots on the floor, our decades-old textbooks. We were supposed to be grateful for the public funds that paid for public schooling, despite the fact that these are our funds, created from the taxes we pay. When we asked for better teaching, more generosity, our parents were implicated for not "teaching at home," for not being "partners to the teacher," for assuming that to teach might also mean "to nurture," and then implicated again for being wrong. The institution protects itself by shifting culpability onto the people it is supposed to be responsible for in every facet of their experience, from their safety to their learning to what happens when they leave the institution and step into the world—with or without an education.

On that first day of high school, I met a girl who was strange in a way that was different from how I was strange. Beautiful, dark-skinned, and short, she navigated the social politics of the classroom with ease. I studied her for the first few days of class, taking subtle cues from her outfits and hairstyles, wondering about this dangerous energy—bright and sad and impulsive— she was carrying around, about whether I had it too.

By the end of the first week of classes, she started to notice me. We became fast friends, and on a random Wednesday, when she asked me what I really wanted to do, what I would do if I could do anything but be in school, I imagined myself sitting somewhere in the warmth of the sun with her, eating a BEC sandwich and laughing and discussing the boy I was dating. I didn't know what the world was like during these hours I never got to see.

I told her all of this and she said, "Let's go." I followed rules because I was told that I had no other option, because there was danger on the other side of a rule.

"We'll sign in and get marked present in third period and then, when security is on break in the red hallway, we'll leave through the back doors. Easy." All the days before this day had gone by metronomically, one period following the other, the rhythms reliable and expected. She was an aberration. Every Wednesday, she'd disappear from fourth period, a disappearance I noticed, and wouldn't return until the next day. I never asked where she went or why she left; it didn't feel like my business. But today, she was inviting me to join her in her elusive escape, to be a partner in this drastic split from reality.

In the third period, I practiced it all in my head—how I was going to back out of leaving, what valid excuse I could give her. By the time the bell rang, I had chickened out. She caught me trying to scurry to my fourth-period class when the bell rang, grabbing me by my belt loop. "Come on," she groaned, pulling me behind her. "We're going."

I ran with my backpack beating against my spine like a pulse, with my two hands out in front of me, punching the lever on the doors with the weight of my entire body, shoving the doors open, flinging them into the wild expanse. We ran so hard our ponytails came loose and we didn't stop until we had made it to the bus stop far up the hill where no security guards were patrolling anymore because it was just the street, no longer the territory of the school. By our own will, we were let free into the void of the world-at-noon, where we could be real people among real people. I felt the sun on my face, that noon sun, such a rare and uncanny feeling, and saw myself and everything around me reflected in the glare of the bus window, tilted.

The world was not as it was at 3 p.m., and 3 p.m. would never be as it had been ever again. Being free at this hour opened a portal in my life that I had dared to step through. I was out in the grown-up world, armed with an ID and a best friend. I could be anything I wanted to be.

That was the first time the world ended for me, as I ran full speed across the threshold of the school doors, running away and into myself. In that first year of high school, I would miss at least 110 out of 180 days, failing the year by default. We spent our days on the streets in a warped universe with other young people who had abandoned the job of being young people. These were all kinds of young people, some much older than others, some who were in and out of jail and homeless shelters, some who had been permanently kicked out of school and forced to test for the GED. There were addicts and dealers and kids with jobs and kids who bounced checks for a living. There were young new mothers and kids whose parents didn't have the capacity to parent them. What we shared was a unique camaraderie organized around the fact that none of us were where we were "supposed" to be, in some ways living outside bourgeois normativity, breaking the rules because they didn't work in our world, weren't relevant to our time. Rebellion had been planted in me like a pomegranate seed.

Breaking the rules was not just a choice of rebellion but a rejection of an American education system that conventionalized institutional harm and the radical loss of sovereignty that all students must undergo to be in line with the institution, to be in the good graces of the institution in order to receive, in return, more access to the institution and the optimisms it draws us toward.

But I was always going to break the rules.

In those streets, I witnessed firsthand the poetry of how we lived, itself a long interrogation of our otherworldliness. We were thinking about what made us different, about why we were living on a different rhythm than everyone else, why we couldn't just be who we were expected to be, why we were othered. We lived outside the conventional present, living outside space and time. To exist at those hours meant that, in some way, we were free. To be outside and alive at those hours meant that we were in conflict with the systematized world, that we lived outside the normative optimisms that everyone else was blindly trapped into. To be in conflict with the edges of time, with the edges of the world, meant that we were in conflict with the enclosure from inside the constraints of the enclosure. In this way, we opened ourselves up to the small blessings that can happen only if you're outside at that hour, like a bus driver waiving someone's fare, the gentle way people greet each other, a particular sad solidarity of being untethered at that time of day, a kinship based on lack or loss.

Outside the walls of where I "belonged," I was able to carve out a different understanding of belonging. My friends and I spent hours on blocks our parents and friends told us to avoid, learning the ecosystems of our neighborhoods, having conversations we wouldn't have been able to have anywhere else. We fell in love with the boys who were deemed dangerous by the world, and found safety in their otherness, felt loved by people whom we were supposed to see as unlovable. Our politics was born from experience, and not just perspective. We were thirteen and fourteen (respectively), picking up our boyfriends—taken in for stolen candy bars—from Central Booking in the middle of the day, thirteen and fourteen at a titi's lunch table learning to prepare a pig for pernil. We were the kinds of kids that some people called bad kids, but we had no shame about our delinquencies, no shame about having escaped. We lived in the fullness of life, outside time, and became who we were going to become under the slow certainty of day.

When I wasn't outside with my friends, I was at home, by myself, surfing the internet and reading books as I watched reruns of *A Different World*. I would buy myself a baguette and a can of tuna from the bodega and eat blissfully as I turned the pages of each book, knowing early what it meant to experience pleasure, what it meant to gift myself, knowing early how to provide myself peace amid the uneasiness of life at home. I sat with myself and came to know myself intimately, cataloging my quirks, identifying what made me different, writing to articulate it all to myself. At twelve I published my first poem, "Purgatory," in a pay-to-play poetry anthology—a clear sign of who I would become, someone stuck in the middle, stuck between someone else's logic and mine.

Between my first year of high school and my fifth, my sense of self and my creativity were developing alongside each other. In secret, far away from my friends and the streets, I would write Harry Potter fan fiction and short stories about girls who wanted and needed to be saved. I was consuming novels, going through at least two a week, reading whenever I could, hiding my books behind math textbooks during class and hiding away in the school libraries, getting suspended for fighting and then using suspension time to read even more. In some ways I was dissociating. In other ways, I was building a practice that would sustain me for a lifetime.

When I was forced to go back to school at the end of the year, and then forced to transfer to another high school to redo my freshman year, I returned feeling even more strange and more different than I had before. I could barely make it through the day without wanting to escape, without wanting to break out of the walls and be that other me who lived on her own terms. It was harder to do at this new, smaller school, which had fewer exits and teachers who actually knew my name. I escaped when I could, but it didn't matter because I had been fundamentally changed by the experience of living outside the metronomic present, because I had read the poetry of the misfits and had become one. Outside my world, everyone seemed to be moving at the same speed, walking to the same tempo. Mine felt disturbed, off-kilter, and inside my world, the misfits were walking to a different beat, breaking the rhythm of the metronome.

I spent time with my mother's collection of classical poetry, and even memorized some poems (at my mother's urging), including Maya Angelou's "Still I Rise" and Langston Hughes's "Harlem." I appreciated classical poetry as a reader but not yet as a writer. I understood, intellectually, the value of its beauty, but not the value of its application.

In eleventh grade my teacher introduced me to Gwendolyn Brooks, and it was one of the few times I was encouraged to think critically about how poetry worked. I was already writing poetry, had already published that weird, elegiac, depressing poem in that pay-to-play anthology. But it wasn't until this encounter with Brooks that I understood what a poem could *do*.

Our teacher, thoughtful and passionate, taught "We Real Cool"* as a sardonic poem, a poem that warned against destructive behavior, that warned about the cost of rebellion—but to me the poem was far from a reprimand. To me the poem said, *Fuck it.* The poem said, *If I gotta go, let me go out fly* and *I sing pleasure's song in the nightmare of my enemy,* and the enemy was not in the room. Freedom's cost was worth it.

To me, this was a poem about seven young people who lived in the fissures of the state, who had the nerve to choose rebellion as a mechanism of survival, who evaded order and suffered death because they could not, or would not, get in order. They

---

* Gwendolyn Brooks, *The Bean Eaters* (Harper, 1960).

didn't simply die, but were killed by the very constraints they escaped.

That same eleventh-grade English teacher, Miss K, read my short fan fictions and poems and told me to really write, with intention, because she thought I was talented and that I needed a push. She recommended that I audition for a youth theater program at MCC Theater, a black box where kids like Amy León and Dominique Fishback were training.

The audition was a series of exercises that we all had to participate in, as either writers or performers. A writer would give a line to an actor to perform, and so on. At the end of the rounds, the mentors went through the crowd of young people and selected twenty students, one by one. When a mentor came to me, I stood there expecting disappointment, until I realized I had gotten in.

Getting into MCC was one of the first times that normalcy—feeling connected rather than needing to escape—felt available to me, and one of the first times my writing had been validated by someone other than my teachers. It turned out that I wasn't very good at acting or writing for theater, not as good as some of the other students, but a couple of months into my work at MCC, I was introduced to a small nonprofit on Twenty-Eighth Street called Urban Word NYC.

I entered their annual teen poetry slam, from which five young people were selected to attend the national poetry slam with hundreds of others from around the country. The first round was preliminaries, and people who placed in preliminaries would move on to semifinals, and so on. The people who placed in the finals would go on to join the national team.

I went to the first slam at the Nuyorican Poets Café with

huge confidence, riding the high of the poem I'd performed to applause for my classmates. There were a lot of kids like me who went onstage, kids who were newer to poetry, and some more experienced, who quickly let me know I was out of my league. I made it to the semifinals but not the finals. I kept attending as a spectator. I had never witnessed expression like this, not online or anywhere else—it blew my mind. The writing coming from these teenagers was crisp and precise. They were talking about abuse, politics, love. They were emoting throughout their poems, moving their bodies with intention, exclaiming onomatopoeias when a word in the poem correlated to the sound of a physical object, like a gunshot or a heartbeat. I left knowing that I needed to be part of that community, with those kids, that kind of art, and those kinds of teachers.

We were so lucky. Incredible, groundbreaking, award-winning poets, many of color, came to Urban Word to hold weekly workshops. Among them were Aracelis Girmay, Mahogany L. Browne, Willie Perdomo, and Patricia Smith.

I continued to learn about poetry there, deepening my study, and I fell even more in love with this genre that filled my life with images and color that I couldn't see before. The mentors at Urban Word taught me how to think about metaphor, syntax, and form. I lapped it up like a thirsty animal, letting it fill me. It helped tremendously that this organization existed outside of school, that I had to take a train downtown to step into this otherworldly space where kids just like me, who knew the dirty side of the day, would all sit at a table to read and write poetry. This was the education I had been looking for.

After becoming immersed in the world of slam poetry, I began to find myself in West Harlem on Sunday afternoons in the living room of the poet and musician Abiodun Oyewole (who also goes by Dun or Pops) of the Last Poets and his good friend Afrikaans. It was one of the few places I was allowed to go on a Sunday, my mother agreeing to it with surprisingly little resistance, that being a small glimmer, a signifier of just how magical and pivotal those experiences would later come to be.

In Dun's house, the cornbread was the law. The greens were the law. The smoke was the law. You did not show up unless you were ready to share—a poem, a plate, a spliff, a song, your energy. Sharing was the law. Learning was the law. You did not show up unless you were willing to sit and interested in sitting at the feet of those principles: of sharing, studying, and self-nourishment. Those places were places I needed to be—Dun's, Urban Word, the Nuyorican—their logics were compulsive and worked well for me. I was with and among family, and I knew this because the laws of their universe bent toward the justice of me and mine and everyone who touched our world, and there was no confusion about whose life was worthy or whose life was valuable and that was a sociopolitical and cultural triumph, a deep promise of what earnest community could be. Mos Def would stop by, Aja Monet is like family to Dun and the Last Poets, and anyone who ever stepped into that room felt the love of family touch them even if they had no blood relation.

Our entry fee, especially if you were a young person, was some artistic offering. If you were a singer, you had to sing. A dancer? You had to dance. A poet, you had to spit in front of this poetry icon and receive his feedback. He and Afrikaans talked in between the poems. The topics always started off with a kind of conspiratorial broadness—*Was the government respon-*

sible for the death of the Black Panther Party? Is the government responsible for all the drug-addicted musicians? Then the topic evolved as the poems got deeper and the conversation became philosophical—*Does our education system have the ability to offer a revolutionary education? Was [insert artwork] good art or was it provocative? Are Black mamas getting the care they need or are we using Black women to offer care in exchange for care?* I learned the most through this weaving, this braiding of genre, tradition, and politics.

I struggled to write sonnets, tankas, and other formal forms. I still do. But formalism in poetry has taught me even more about how a poem writes itself into and out of constraint—shape, meter, line length, and other rules—as a kind of fugitivity. Knowing the rules, after all, is about breaking them. In order to complicate tradition, poets engage with it, confront it. When we write out of the constraint and break the order of the poem, something is set free in the poem. Black poets especially have taken form to task, have broken it open and sutured it back together, giving it new skin, new rules, new relevance. Take for instance the sonnet. Translated from the Italian word *sonetto*, meaning "little song," the sonnet is traditionally a fourteen-line poem written in iambic pentameter that might often rhyme, ending with a volta, the final moment in the poem where the resolution completely disrupts the meaning and feeling.

Wanda Coleman broke through and out of the sonnet in her work. Typical were disruptions of lineation, where one vertical line would feature multiple lines set apart by slashes. In this way, she keeps the tradition of a fourteen-line sonnet but breaks the rules by having multiple little lines of the poem occupy the vertical line on the page.

Coleman was dismissed by an editor who called her work, derisively, jazz poetry. "Since jazz is an open form with certain properties—progression, improvisation, mimicry, etcetera, I decided that likewise the jazz sonnet would be as open as possible, adhering only to the loosely followed dictate of number of lines," Coleman told Paul Nelson in 2002. "I decided on fourteen to sixteen and to not exceed that, but to go absolutely bonkers within that constraint. I also give the sonnets a jazzified rhythm structure, akin to platter patter and/or scat and tones like certain Beat writers. . . . I decided to have fun—to blow my soul."* Coleman reached back toward the meat of what was intended as an insult to come up with the rules that would produce a new kind of sonnet; her book *American Sonnets* was published in 1994. Coleman is a fugitive of the form, breaking away from it compulsively, broken away from it by force. When the racist editor attempted to demean her work by demeaning the very essence of her work, Coleman went back to that essence and centered it in her practice, running up against tradition, her work showing us her aim to confront Shakespeare's with a version of her own. The form is not the vehicle of the poem. The form is only the container. The Black poet breaks out of the container by design. Because she must. Because she is left with no choice.

---

* Wanda Coleman, "Subject: American Sonnets." Interview by Paul Nelson in *American Prophets: Interviews with Thinkers, Activists, Poets and Visionaries* (Splab!, 2019).

For artists, this is how we learn—through active consumption and constant production. It happens as much in isolation as it does among the powerful, communal influence of a collective. It would be twenty years before I learned long division, but at least I knew what allegory was, and I knew how to understand tragedy as a literary event, and I knew what an epic was and how one long verse in narrative form could turn the Bible into a Greek tragedy. The alienation I felt within educational institutions shaped itself into an instinct that brought me closer to the education that would shape my worldviews, my political impulses, my social optimisms. The institution prepared me through negation: by making me feel that I existed outside it and couldn't be contained by it, naturally, I came to agree. Through this suggestion, I was able to gather the critical and fundamental pieces of myself into an authentic sense of knowing, the very sense of knowing that led me to this place of ultimate frustration and disillusionment with the institution of education and with all governing institutions that dictate and organize how we exist within a shared, burdened sociality. Rebellion was my liberation.

Excerpt from No Child Left Behind

██████████████████████████████████
██████████████████████████████████
██████████████████████████████████
████████████████████

██████████████████████████████████
███████████████████████████████ as-
sessments of ████████████████
agency ███████████████████████
████████████ to ██████████████████
██████████████████████████████████
█████████████████████████
██████████████████████████████████
██████████████████████████████████
████████████████

████████ define █████████████████
██████████████████████████████████
████████████████████████

██████████████████████████████████
███████████████████████████████ the
██████████████████████████████████
██████████████████████████████████
██████████████████████████████████
██████████████████████████████████
emergency █████████████████████████
██████████████████████████████████

LET THE POETS GOVERN - 61

that fails,

the State's plan

, unless

the practicable

priority

is

instruction

action

relevant to the

promise

of

precipitous

opportunity to

achieve

alter-
native   governance and

Limit

loss.

CHAPTER 4

THE SUGAR

Grenada has its own smell. Before the plane cabin let me loose into the country's small, warm body, I smelled its sweat. Nutmeg, coconut, the sharp scent of ocean salt carrying the wet sweetness of sugarcane. As my father and I were driven away from the airport, the colors of the landscape began to materialize with the slow urgency that marks the nature of Caribbean life: along the one main road, the small homes and standing structures that house the people, the animals, and the culture of this remarkable land. I was eight and had never felt this before—a sense of calm bliss, the kind impossible to find in a city of walls.

I come from many generations of Grenadians brought to the island by a legacy that has defined our relationship to the land. Its indigenous* names are Kamahuya and Camáhogne. The first means "thunderbolt" and the other "conception" in Arawak and Kalinago. My parents combined these to create my name, Camonghne. I am "thunderbolt conception," a strike of light, an immaculate conception.

On my trip to Grenada, my father cut a piece of sugarcane flesh—just a bite, small enough to chew whole—and pushed it into my mouth. At first I was shocked by its density and the plainness of the fibers. But then I bit down, the cane broke in the grind of my teeth, and just as a child would, I chewed in delight—pure sugar in my mouth.

We put sugar in everything. Sugar in our tea, sugar in our milk, sugar in our dumplings, sugar in our porridge, sugar in our grits.

"You eat too much sugar," my dad would complain as I sucked on a random piece of candy he'd picked up on his travels, bought just for me. "It's going to ruin your teeth."

He was right. I don't have great teeth. Four teaspoons of sugar in my mint tea every morning. Four teaspoons of a spice that designed me. Somewhere in history, a person with my eyes, or perhaps my nose, or perhaps my average-size feet bled into the sugar crop that funded the very democracies that violate me. Somewhere in the midst of history, a person with my hands ripped their hands apart as they stripped the

---

* The word "indigenous" itself is an example of how language inflicts violence without trying. The construct of indigeneity defines people's origins in response to colonial power. Without adequate language, we are forced to replicate the systems of erasure that trap us into that dynamic.

sugar crop that funded their enslavement. That is the irony that offends me.

It was after Columbus arrived in the Caribbean that the island was named La Concepción. The naming is ironic; it is named as if it came out of nowhere, as if it hadn't already existed. After the French came to settle on the island, they named it La Grenada and worked to eliminate the native population. On May 30, 1650, Chief Kairouane of the native Kalinago people and more than forty of his men jumped from Leapers Hill in the northernmost part of Grenada in a mass suicide. Eventually historians came to question whether it was suicide or murder, whether the Kalinago people jumped or were pushed over the edge as a consequence for noncompliance.* Either way, the Hill is a monument to resistance. Grenada's land is charged with this history. While most estimates are inaccurate, it is said that more than a hundred thousand Africans were kidnapped and sent to Grenada during the Middle Passage.

The Christian Bible was perhaps the original document that granted permission for the countless crimes committed in the long tale of European colonization. As an object, the Bible is not itself inherently problematic or violent, but written as a poem is written, with encouragement to ponder on the various interpretations, leaving it up to the reader or listener to relate to

---

* J. A. Martin, "We Navel-String Bury Here: Landscape History, Representation and Identity in the Grenada Islandscape" (PhD diss., Leiden University, 2023).

it in whatever way they must in order to react to its call, it can be experienced as violent. As an object, it is a permit in the same way that a driving permit is issued, in the same way that a parking permit is issued—it suggests that a grand authority has sanctioned the interpretation and endorsed it, giving the image permission to come through.

It is the story of Noah's curse, the tale in Genesis 9:18–29. In the common interpretation of the story of Ham, Noah cursed Ham's son Canaan as punishment for Ham's looking upon his father Noah's naked body as he slept after the floodwaters retreated. The implication spreads and seeps into Ham's descendants: They are uncivilized, and thus bastardized, becoming lifelong slaves of their brothers, Ham's progeny cursed in perpetuity.

God condemns Ham's lineage to an eternity of captivity, endorsing slavery as a valid progression of consequence. The Bible never mentions the color of Ham's skin, but by the nineteenth century, as the story of Ham made its way throughout the Judeo-Christian and Arab worlds, the interpretation of it evolved into a theory and belief that Black people were the descendants of Ham.

This interpretation is an entirely made-up concept that European colonizers weaponized to establish a racial hierarchy that would justify the siege and exploitation of Africans. White southern Christians were especially interested in this interpretation, happy to believe that Black people were meant to be "perpetual" slaves. The Bible, which began as a text meant to define morality, became a legal document when its poetics proved exploitable by the European colonial powers who relied on the Word to bolster their claims to the land and people they'd stolen.

On that first trip to Grenada, I, against all recommendations and warnings, insisted on wearing the gray leather Barbie pants I got for my birthday that year. My dad told me it would be too hot. My mom told me it would be too hot. My grandmother kissed her teeth and looked away, folding her hands into the crooks of her arms as Caribbean grandmothers do when their noir-generationed grandchildren approach the island like tourists, bug-eyed as they try to adjust to the unfamiliar. The pants were in fact too hot to wear on an 88-degree day on an island surrounded by the sea.

I was a tourist for the first twenty-four hours of the trip. But in the days that followed I became part of the island's biorhythm. I played with the kids who lived down the road. I learned to climb a tree. I learned to squash mosquitoes and sandflies. I learned to swim. I walked barefoot on dirt and suffered the tiny bites and great red swelling of a tragic encounter with fire ants—I was stepping on their anthill and they wanted me to move. I sucked passion fruit with my cavities, my face pulled in by its tart juice as I watched my great-aunt kill the ticks hiding in the family dog's fur with a beer bottle cap, hearing the soft *pop-pop-pop* of the tiny blood-sucking insects.

I watched my beautiful cousins prepare for carnival fetes in Caricou, a boat ride away, my eldest cousin kissing my face softly and promising that she'd take me *onto di road* when I was of age.

In Merle Collins's *Because the Dawn Breaks!: Poems Dedicated to the Grenadian People,* the poem "Callaloo" harnesses the singsong tone that defines Grenadian patois.* The poem synthesizes the revolution's energy and its necessity in these tight stanzas, sometimes just one syllable a line, that articulate the unique dialect of the Grenadian people. These are the language and accent given to me:

> An' wid you head in de air
> becus de world is yours
> an' you know is yours
> an' you not goin' be
> meek
> meek
> meek
> an' wait to see
> if
> somebody
> goin' let you
> inherit the earth
> becus you know arready
> is yours

What was the material of this small, enigmatic island? What gave its people such a sense of freedom, such lyrical ways of being and walking and seeing? What kind of turn made it Eden?

The network of ownership of Grenada grew as time went on, the French handing the island over to Britain in 1783. Euro-

---

* Merle Collins, *Because the Dawn Breaks!: Poems Dedicated to the Grenadian People* (Karia Press, 1985).

pean colonialists were the assumed "owners," and then, in 1823, the U.S. asserted its "rights" over Grenada (and the rest of Latin America and the Caribbean) when President James Monroe articulated a new foreign policy that came to be known as the Monroe Doctrine. Monroe believed that the U.S. had power to claim the entire Caribbean basin as theirs to police. This policy made Grenada a target and, more than a hundred years later, gave the U.S. a channel by which to access Cuba in its pursuit to quell communism. This tiny 133-square-mile island—a destabilizing threat. This was the state of affairs until the burgeoning independence movements of the 1950s arose.

In 1791, in the French island colony formerly known as Saint-Domingue, now Haiti, Toussaint L'Ouverture led a rebellion that would make freedom from the tyrannical powers of Europe an infectious reality, overthrowing French rule and becoming the first successful abolitionist revolt of Black slaves in history. (The earliest revolt was in today's Dominican Republic, Haiti's neighbor, as early as 1521.) Its echo was heard by the enslaved on every island within the Caribbean Basin, moving through the waters until it made its way to the Grenadian shores.

A young Grenadian later known as Henri Christophe became one of the leaders of the Haitian Revolution after growing into maturity by fighting in the critical Battle of Savannah in the American Revolution at twelve years old.

In 1795, Grenada chose to stand firm on one uncompromising demand: freedom. Though the 1795 revolt ended differently than the 1791 actions in Haiti, the Grenadian people had forever changed the DNA of resistance on the island. This unfiltered revolutionary praxis later inspired Grenada's ten thousand agriculture workers to rise up against Britain's colonial rule in a

1951 strike, an early salvo in the path toward independence. The resistance came together in the New Jewel Movement, established in 1973, a "Marxist Leninist vanguard party" organized by Maurice Bishop and others. A year later, Grenada finally achieved independence from Britain, leading to its first democratic election. In the end, the Grenada United Labour Party won 71 percent of the vote and Eric Gairy, the son of a plantation overseer in St. Andrew and erstwhile leader of the 1951 revolt, became Grenada's first prime minister.

Still, even after the establishment of Grenada's democratic government, Grenada continued to live under the foot of Western imperialism in this neocolonial framework. Gairy was a pro-imperialist who believed in Grenada's reliance on the support of the U.S. Many Grenadians saw this position as a betrayal of the Grenadian people who had resisted only to end up back in the clutches of imperial power. The noise that Haiti's two revolutions had made had not yet been excised from the DNA of the Caribbean people. The people of Grenada were hungry. They were exploited. They were poor and angry.

The New Jewel Movement continued its organizing work, and on March 13, 1979, NJM ousted Eric Gairy in a people's own revolutionary coup against Gairy's government, launched while Gairy was away on a visit to the U.S. The movement took control of the military, the police stations, the government buildings, and the radio stations—a brilliant execution of revolutionary praxis—establishing the People's Revolutionary Government.

My dad is an artist who contributed to the Grenadian revolution and the movement, and though he would never call himself a poet, I've seen him write plenty of poems and short stories, all in some way informed by the world he became an adult in—the split world of revolution in Grenada and the austerity and frigid dehumanization of Black people in the United States. The revolution was hopeful; it meant for my dad that his readings of Freire and Foucault, Fanon and McKay, Marx and Césaire were useful, that there was something to apply from his readings, that it wasn't just theory.

NEW JEWEL MOVEMENT MANIFESTO

The people are being cheated and have been cheated for too long—cheated by both parties, for over twenty years. Nobody is asking what the people want. We suffer low wages and higher cost of living while the politicians get richer, live in bigger houses and drive around in even bigger cars. The government has done nothing to help people build decent houses; most people still have to walk miles to get water to drink after 22 years of politicians.

If we fall sick we catch hell to get quick and cheap medical treatment. Half of us can't find steady work. The place is getting from bad to worse every day—except for the politicians (just look at how they dress and how they move around). The police are being used in politics these days and people are getting more and more blows from them. Government workers who don't toe the Gairy line are getting fired left and right. Even the magistrates better look out!

The government has no idea how to improve agriculture, how to set up industries, how to improve housing, health, education and general well-being of the people. They have no ideas for helping the people. All they know is how to take the people's money for themselves, while the people scrape and scrunt for a living.

We believe that the main concern of us all is to (1) prevent the daily rise in prices of all our food and clothes and other essentials (it is unbelievable but true that the price you can get for a pound of cocoa can't buy a half-pound of fish) and (2) develop a concrete program for raising the standard of housing, living, education, health, food and recreation for all the people.

The present situation we face is that we are forced to live in jammed-up, rundown, unpainted houses without toilet and bath, without running water, very poor roads, overcrowded schools where our children can't get a decent education, and without any proper bus service. There is almost no ambulance service in case of illness. We can't afford the cost of food to feed our children properly and this makes it easier for them to catch all kinds of illnesses. There are very few places near home for recreation. All we have is the rumshop to drown our troubles. It's almost impossible to buy clothes or shoes these days. The prices are ridiculous.

Twenty years of the GNP and the GULP have made us believe that there is no way out of this blasted mess. BUT THERE IS, and the time is NOW to do something about it.[*]

---

[*] "The New Jewel Revolution in Grenada," NACLA Report on the Americas (1980).

The stakes are clear; the manifesto tells the people "there is no time left to continue this way" and counts what has been lost.

The manifesto, with its precise and unwieldy tone, put teeth to what must come next, revolution. The soil was fertile and thirsty. This document antagonizes all documents that led to the need for one. There is no "vanquish" or "removal" here. There is "decency," there is "concern." It's proof of language's capacity to mobilize. It's what revolution is supposed to do, send out millions of mirrors to confirm that it can be done, that you can stand up against the loud noise of corruption and colonization to free yourself and your people.

The movement's insurrection launched tiny Grenada into national recognition. The party established free healthcare, free milk and school lunches, free secondary education, loans for housing, exemptions from income tax for some workers, maternity leave for women, and more. Like any revolutionary government, it had its faults. It was young and independent from the parentage of world powers, but it was most successful at raising anti-imperialist class consciousness. Those faults, though, made the island vulnerable to the exploitation of those very Western powers, and in 1983, the island was invaded by the U.S. on the pretext of restoring democratic governance and isolating it from communist influence. At an annual meeting of the National Association of Manufacturers, in March of that same year, Reagan clearly says to the room his intentions for the Spice Island:

> Grenada, that tiny little island—with Cuba at the west end of the Caribbean, Grenada at the east end—that tiny little island

is building now, or having built for it, on its soil and shores, a naval base, a superior air base, storage bases and facilities for the storage of munitions, barracks, and training grounds for the military. I'm sure all of that is simply to encourage the export of nutmeg.

People who make these arguments haven't taken a good look at a map lately or followed the extraordinary buildup of Soviet and Cuban military power in the region or read the Soviets' discussions about why the region is important to them and how they intend to use it.

It isn't nutmeg that's at stake in the Caribbean and Central America; it is the United States' national security.*

All of these claims made by Reagan were proven to be lies, not unlike some of the ridiculous claims of Trump today.

On October 19, 1983, Maurice Bishop was overthrown and murdered by firing squad after a successful coup led by Deputy Prime Minister Bernard Coard.

Only six days later, on October 25, 1983, a new radio station began broadcasting from a U.S. Navy ship, demanding that Cubans leave the island and that Grenadians open their homes to American forces. Soldiers ran through Grenada, wheat-pasting propaganda posters on the walls. From the sky, helicopters dropped leaflets that attempted to persuade citizens to support the coming invasion. Then, in the twilight hours, a small group of U.S. Marines landed on Grenadian soil, launching an inva-

---

* "Remarks on Central America and El Salvador at the Annual Meeting of the National Association of Manufacturers," 1983.

sion code-named Operation Urgent Fury and capturing several airstrips.

> **CITIZENS OF GRENADA**
>
> TAKE EVERY PRECAUTION TO INSURE YOUR SAFETY. HELP US AVOID ACCIDENTALLY INJURING YOU OR YOUR FAMILIES BY TAKING THE FOLLOWING STEPS:
> 1. DO NOT LEAVE YOUR HOME
> 2. AVOID CONFRONTATIONS AND DO NOT INTERFER WITH U.S./CARIBBEAN FORCES
> 3. IF FIGHTING STARTS IN YOUR AREA STAY IN YOUR HOMES AND ON THE FLOOR
> 4. STAY OFF ROADS AND HIGHWAYS
> 5. FURTHER EMERGENCY INFORMATION WILL FOLLOW
>
> PLEASE REMAIN CALM AND NO HARM WILL COME TO YOU.

> **CITIZENS OF GRENADA**
>
> TAKE EVERY PRECAUTION TO INSURE YOUR SAFETY.
> HELP US AVOID ACCIDENTALLY INJURING YOU OR MEMBERS OF YOUR FAMILIES BY TAKING THE STEPS ON THE REVERSE SIDE.
> PLEASE REMAIN CALM AND NO HARM WILL COME TO YOU.

On the ground, amid the intense bombing and home invasions, the Americans launched a 50-kilowatt broadcast news station, Spice Island Radio, with their first broadcast demanding that Grenadians relinquish their arms. U.S. trucks on Grenadian roads boomed psyops* messaging: "Help protect your hard-fought freedom," it said. "Send the Cubans back to Havana where they belong."

The invasion would be met with strong resistance, and fighting would continue until Friday, October 28, with an estimated 19 U.S. soldiers killed and 115 wounded; 25 Cubans killed, 59 wounded; and 45 Grenadians killed, 358 wounded.

While this operation could not kill the spirit of revolution in Grenada, it did suppress it by force. In the following year, the

---

* A psyops, or psychological operations, unit is a military unit focused on using psychological influence to achieve objectives, typically through nonlethal means. These units aim to persuade, influence, or deceive foreign audiences to support military goals. They use a variety of techniques, including the dissemination of information, messages, and actions, to achieve their objectives.

U.S. would continue to drop propaganda on the island to maintain support for the invasion and to subdue any attempts at the seeding of a new revolutionary party. One such piece of propaganda was a fourteen-page comic book titled *Grenada: Rescued from Rape and Slavery*. The irony speaks for itself. The white savior of the West comes to liberate Grenada from its own liberation, with language as the tool in place of direct force.

Grenada's revolution was a splinter in this history, causing the U.S. and the U.K. governments to use actual imperial force to subdue the radicality of a small island of just over a hundred thousand people. Grenada, like many other countries in Latin America and the Caribbean, became, once again, the victim of American imperial ambitions, a geopolitical tool of Western superpowers. American colonial imperialism reveals itself as the pervasive force that it is, its perversions traced through history, vehicled by the language that surrounds and defends it.

On June 5, 1983, Maurice Bishop, in a singular and stirring speech at Hunter College in New York City, says to his majority Black audience: "They said that 95 percent of our population is Black, and they had a correct statistic. And if we have 95 percent of predominantly African origin in our country, then we can have a dangerous appeal to thirty million Black people in the United States."*

In *The Wretched of the Earth,* the Black Caribbean poet and revolutionary philosopher Frantz Fanon says, "We could go on to portray the rise of a new nation, the establishment of a new state, its diplomatic relations and its economic and political orientation. But instead we have decided to describe the kind of tabula rasa which from the outset defines any decolonization."

He warns that decolonization and the command to move into a new state of organization require the colonized to completely reimagine the social fabric that defines our current state, from the inside out. They must be demanded and clamored for.

Grenada began again from a tabula rasa when the New Jewel Movement's manifesto was spoken into the world by a community of Black workers who knew that whatever power structure should exist would be one dedicated to meeting the needs of the people. The imagination of the People's Revolutionary Government went much further than Gairy's—instead of capitulating to the colonizer's demands, they focused on building new international diplomatic relations, including the establishment of a relationship with the Republic of Cuba.

In 2016, I sat across from Angela Davis in Florence, Italy, where we were both speakers at New York University Florence's

---

* Maurice Bishop, "Maurice Bishop Speaks in NYC at Hunter College," June 5, 1983, Internet Archive, archive.org/details/maurice-bishop-speaks.

Agenda for Black Femininity Series. Her soft honeyed hair gleamed in contrast to the stark white of the tablecloth, her Afro trembling as she spoke, her impassioned voice being the cadence of its movement. I wondered if she had ever been to Grenada—and of course she had. She told me about its splendor and described the wonder she felt as she was witnessing Grenada's revolution. It makes sense what she saw. The world, when they looked down at their morning papers, saw Grenada's resistance and attempted to name it. Something miraculous had happened in Grenada, something fugitive and insolent. It was almost magical, an echo of the sound that Haiti had made.

The list of Grenadian and other Caribbean contributions to U.S. revolutionary and civil rights struggles is well-known. Malcolm X's mother, for example, was born in Saint Andrew Parish, Grenada. The socialists Kwame Ture and Claudia Jones are from Trinidad. The socialist labor leader Ferdinand Smith is from Jamaica.

With revolution as a lexicon for the colonized in the Caribbean, from the fields to parliament, the legacy of colonization could not be stamped out of the islands' political composition. And so the need for the People's Revolution was and remains a great antiracist, anticolonial practice in the struggle.

You can find the mark of this kind of revolutionary praxis all across the Caribbean and Latin America, where Black and Afro-Caribbean folks organize to overthrow the metropole in order to form their governance. These struggles mirrored, in many ways, the same struggles that Black folks everywhere, especially in the Americas, faced. Similarly, while that resistance was significant to the ongoing fight for an antiracist society and has brought Black and Brown people some material gain, capitalism remains a disruptive force that traffics in the images of freedom while denying it in fact.

Sugar, the milk of my belonging, is the substance that links me to the South and links the South to the Caribbean and links the Caribbean to Britain and links Britain to the founders of democracy, which brings democracy full circle as the matrix of colonial violence. The poetry of my own subjugation had been planted in my mouth, planted for me to repeat and perpetuate. The South is in my mouth. The Caribbean is in my mouth. Latin America is in my mouth.

During my first and only trip to Grenada, a story of many first-generation Caribbean immigrants, I saw jab-jab—a tradition dating back to slavery in which Grenadians paint their bodies in molasses, tar, black paint, engine oil, or chocolate to symbolize and embody the revolutionary spirit of the enslaved on the sugar plantation—for the first time during J'ouvert, the celebration that marks the official start of Carnival. The term "jab-jab" comes from the French word *diable*, which means "devil." During jab-jab, Grenadians skin their teeth[*] and dance with machetes in hand, an intentionally violent image that reflects the island's history of rebellion. This image, in its essence, makes a mockery of the story of Ham and the colonial powers' translation. How could a people doomed to subjugation be so good at resisting it? This image proves that revolution is a birthright, and that the colonizer should fear the people's resistance forever.

---

[*] "Skin their teeth" is a patois term that means to smile or grin.

Remarks on Central America and El Salvador at the Annual Meeting of the National Association of Manufacturers

LET THE POETS GOVERN - 81

today I'd like to report to you

the strategic stakes are high

Here—[referring to a map]—

is

the

lesson

New aspirations have emerged

the threat

is

the

nutmeg.

LET THE POETS GOVERN - 83

is

the extraordinary buildup of

our capacity

to

notice:

they've written about this

in ways th a t

■ replace ■ ■ the politics of death with ■ democracy. ■ the good news is that ■ freedom ■ is the clear choice ■

The bad news is that ■ these are not ■ irregulars; they ■

LET THE POETS GOVERN

███████████████████████████████████
███████████████████████████████████
███████████████████████████████████
███████████████████████████████████
███████████████████████████████████
███████████████████████████████████
███████████████████████████████████
████████████████████

███████████████████████████████████
███████████████████████████████████
███████████████████████████████████
███████████████████████████████████
███████████████████████████████████
███████████████████████████████████
█████████████████████████ use
democratic means ██████████████████
████████████ to terror, sabotage, and bullet ███
█ the ballot ███
███████████████████████████████████
███████████████████████████████████
███████████████████████████████████
████████████
███████████████████████████████████
███████████████████████████████████
███████████████████████████████████
████████████████████ But ██████████
███████████████████████████████████
███████████████████████████████████

███████████████ the moment ██
████████████████████████████
████████████████ is running out.
████████████████████████████
████████ the answer ██ is a flat no.
████████████████████████████
██████████████████
████████████████████████████
████████████████████████████
████████████████████████████
████████████████████████████
████████████████████████████
████████████████████████████
████████████████████████████
████████████████████████████
████████████████████████████
████████████████████████████
████████████████████████████
████████████████████████████
████████████████████████████
████████████████████████████
████████████████████████████
████████████████████████████
████████████████████████████
████████████████████████████
████████████████████████████
████████████████████████████
████████████████████████████
████ The real solution ████████

LET THE POETS GOVERN - 87

is

subversion

we oppose negotiations that

distribute power among

government

s.

the legitimate

road is

███████████████████████████████████████ a
practical belief that ▮ free people ███████
███
███
███
████████████████████████████████
███
███
███
███
███
███
███
███
███
██████████████████████████████
███
███
███
███
███
███
                    can defend ███████
███
███
███
███████████
█████████████████████████ human rights,
███

LET THE POETS GOVERN

And we will provide it.

And we will

build a stable

Peace

that

n o

one

poll

LET THE POETS GOVERN — 91

can

measure

understand

that

none of this will work if we tire

our

traditions ▮▮▮ Our ▮▮▮ struggle for ▮▮▮
▮▮▮▮▮▮▮▮▮▮▮▮
▮▮▮
▮▮▮▮▮▮▮▮▮▮
▮▮▮ the great potential ▮▮▮
▮▮▮▮▮▮▮▮▮ of
▮▮▮▮▮▮▮▮▮▮▮▮
▮▮▮▮▮▮▮▮▮▮▮▮
▮▮▮▮▮▮▮▮▮
▮▮▮▮▮▮▮▮▮▮
▮▮▮▮▮▮▮▮▮▮▮▮
▮▮▮▮▮▮▮▮▮▮▮▮
▮▮▮▮▮▮▮▮▮▮▮▮
▮▮▮▮▮▮▮▮▮▮▮▮
▮▮▮▮▮▮▮▮▮▮▮▮
▮▮▮▮▮▮▮▮▮
▮▮▮ our ▮▮▮
▮▮▮ neighbors, ▮▮▮
▮▮▮▮▮▮▮▮▮▮▮▮
▮▮▮▮▮▮▮▮▮▮
▮▮▮ a ▮▮▮
▮▮▮ partnership ▮▮▮
▮▮▮▮▮▮▮▮▮
▮▮▮▮▮▮▮▮▮▮▮▮
▮▮▮▮▮▮▮▮▮▮ founded
on the respect ▮▮▮
▮▮▮▮▮▮ of ▮▮▮ the
▮▮▮ common ▮▮▮
▮▮▮ s we ▮▮▮

LET THE POETS GOVERN - 93

▓▓▓ pledge ▓▓▓ to ▓▓▓ achieve a ▓▓ just ▓▓▓ future. And ▓▓▓ stand true to ▓▓ the ▓▓ values of our ▓▓▓ vital interests.

CHAPTER 5

THE ORDER

In 2011, when I began organizing, I came to it with questions about the politics of bodies and of what it meant to put one's physical being on the line. I wanted to invest in direct action with the politics of disruption. Really, I began with agitation. I didn't fully understand the history of organizing, or the impact it has had on the trajectory of history. I wanted immediate satisfaction, for each protest to lead to direct and swift change, for the state to hear our cries and consider a newfound empathy.

I knew that social change and political change were limbs on the same body, but I thought that organizing couldn't be successful unless it could work within the bounds of our legislative constraints. I knew that our collective voices and collective power were real, but I thought that that power couldn't be useful unless it was augmenting the "insider" strategy.

But soon I found that I wanted to be in control of the apparatus that could execute change. Even the word "execute" speaks to the violence of dominance and control. I wanted change to be a car steered by the drivers we had, because *What other choice do we have?* I was consenting to abuse and consenting to becoming a participant by wanting control, and then by giving it away.

In 2016, after Trump had filed for the presidency, activists and leftists were torn over the question of whether we should vote for Hillary Clinton after she beat Bernie Sanders out for the Democratic nomination. Leftists were sore and angry, Black activists felt they had no choice but to vote for the Democratic nominee, and people from both groups questioned whether we should vote at all. Facebook was the primary social media space for most people, and there were so many different perspectives weighing in on the debate. The question of representation was ripe then: Should we elect a woman and prove to the world that a woman could lead? Should we vote up and down the ballot for less than ideal candidates who would sell Black people out as soon as politically expedient? Should we vote with the hope that more and more progressive Democrats would show up eventually if we just stuck with the Dem platform?

I remember telling the author and overall hero of a human Kiese Laymon that we *had* to vote because it was the only access we had to true political power, because state elections have the most direct impact on our day-to-day lives, because we

Camonghne Felix
June 3, 2016

"Their legacy is very much your vision and your legacy." - Michelle Obama who speaks on the four fathers and how while they never intended to include us, their vision belongs to us too. Which is why I pushed back when the awesome Kiese Laymon said "let no black child run for president again" because without us, without the desire to insert ourselves, include ourselves, without our desire to actively change the status quo, we will continue to see the rest of the nation benefit from privileges that we have to cry and die for. I'm tired of crying. I'm tired of dying. I'm here to do the work.

If this legacy of peace, freedom, prosperity, does not belong to you - the descendants of slave hands that built the White House - who does it belong to.

Claim it. It's yours.

couldn't let "the other side" win and make things worse for all of us. I wrote on Facebook:

I was, in essence, afraid, and I was made to be afraid. All the fearmongering messaging worked on me, and the fearmongering messaging turned out to be right. I was afraid of Trump, of the implications of Trump, of the institution that Trump would become. I was terrified that he would win the presidency, and that the world I lived in would be *more* violent, *more* unsafe, *more* disenfranchising. This felt like the crisis. He was, of course, and remains, a garbage and dangerously persistent human being. But fear is a language that our politics speaks well. Our politics runs on fear, our votes are motivated by fear, our governments govern in response to fear. Our politics manufactures fear and manipulates us into crisis as a way to keep the crisis alive. It's not that there's nothing to be afraid of. Of course, there is much.

When the poet engages fear, she does so knowing all of the above, that fear lives in the pen, and that it can be deployed to elicit response and to initiate action. In fact, the poet knows best the utility of fear; when the poem traffics in it, the poem takes on a life of its own, living in the consciousness of the reader long after the first encounter. In her poem "Allowables," Nikki Giovanni observes:[*]

> . . . only a small
> Sort of papery spider
> Who should have run

In this poem, fear is a channel that takes the poem toward a moral question, which is *Am I allowed to kill something?* In response to that question, the speaker of the poem describes "smashing" the spider, which tells us that we give ourselves permission to kill something when we are "frightened." The poem qualifies its violence at the very beginning, then lets the reader know that this justification is invalid. We are not allowed to kill something because we are afraid. But people do. Nations do. And both use fear as an apparatus of control.

When our bodies feel fear, it's a response to the brain, which is trying to keep us safe from harm. But when fear becomes a tactical weapon, when it becomes a tool of persuasion, that is when the questions arise as to whom the fear is meant to keep safe. Fear, when used as a weaponization of affect, is intended to induce anxiety. At the root of fanaticism is fear. At the root of xenophobia is fear. At the root of nationalism is fear.

Optimism, which the left and the right of our politics use, is also cultivated as a response to fear. Optimism is rooted in the notion that if the voter's chosen hero can beat an opposing candidate whose agenda they are fearful of, then we'll be saved and everything will remain normal. This notion is deceptive. The

---

[*] Nikki Giovanni, *Chasing Utopia: A Hybrid* (William Morrow, 2016).

voter is actually getting not a vision of the future, but a vision of the status quo, which opposes what they fear. That kind of optimism tells us we will be saved if we accept the savior, but the savior has no fidelity to the people who most need that optimism. Inertia is the math of an election, where the voter is unsure of how to continue to participate in the political process without fear as a motivator.

Fear is most often deployed through the rhetoric and semantics of political campaigns, with an intentional absence of focus on policy. From campaign ads to speeches, fear is the language, as Biden's campaign illustrated in his 2020 "battle for the soul of the nation."

Because of that fear, I spent so many hours in 2016 trying to convince my more skeptical friends that the insider-outsider framework, the parallel track of influencing policy from inside the house while relying on others to bring the fight to the government's front door, was the right and only way to fight. I told them that fixing the political body was like fixing a real body, that there would need to be a topical application of medicine and a surgical intervention. I told them that I wanted to be the surgeon.

Slowly, incrementalism was wearing on me. I stopped believing that change could be radical. I argued that ethnic representation was the only key to political access. I was sure that the political system we'd inherited was all there could be, that it was inescapable; we had to become good stewards of democracy. I argued that Black people needed to follow the rules of engagement in order to play the game and that we should aspire to have a seat at the big table of democratic negotiation in order to make it into the negotiation package. As bell hooks says,*

> No insurgent intellectual, no dissenting critical voice in this society escapes the pressure to conform. . . . We can all be had, co-opted, bought. There is no special grace that rescues any of us.

Yes. As designed, I had been gaslighted into oblivion by the foot on my neck.

Kiese wrote back:

Kiese Laymon
I so hear you. I apologize for not being clear before. My worry and fear are that we have to morally bankrupt ourselves to occupy a seat as the head of Empire. And, as we see with Obama, the person will have to bear the weight of the worst of white fokls. There are just some jobs I don't want black people I love to occupy, and the tricky part is that I know that we need brave, brilliant, loving people in those positions. So yeah, I agree with you. I was just also pushing back against how I was raised. When I was kid, white folks kept telling us we could one day be President, which meant, that we could one day be like them. I just think there are so many more incredible jobs in addition to President, you know? And I know folks hate when I say this, but I think Obama could have done far more for us if he wasn't President. But yeah, I hear every word you're saying. I want to live in a world where you are my President. But I'm afraid of what this world has done, is doing, would do to President Felix's insides and outsides.

Like   Reply   7y   8

Youth is the asylum of half-truths. It is true that legislative change is incremental within our legislative apparatus. It is true that representation has become the key to access. It is true that Hillary Clinton was among the best we could do.

---

* bell hooks and Cornel West, *Breaking Bread: Insurgent Black Intellectual Life* (Routledge, 2016).

I was wrong, mostly, about everything else.

Around this time of contemplation, I had been working within the BLM movement, running We Declare Genocide, when I started to feel that this work wasn't moving fast enough, that results were not happening with the urgency they required. I started to feel that the solution might not be in the streets, but somewhere within the apparatus that had created the conditions of this violence. I heard from an aide to the lead counsel for Governor Andrew Cuomo that the governor had been searching for a speechwriter who was also a poet. The counsel's assistant read through my social media posts and coverage of the protests I'd organized. When I spoke to the counsel herself, we discussed my politics, my organizing history, the work I'd done during the Trayvon Martin uprisings, the political nature of my poems, my public persona. None of it was a surprise to her, as she'd had her assistant prescreen me before we spoke. She seemed unfazed. She did not take me seriously, but she knew she could make use of me. She asked me why I wanted to work for the governor. I told her that I wanted to understand how policymaking worked, and how poetry could make policy work better. She offered me the position on the spot. With what seemed like amusement, she told me that my posts about protests and my tweets that called cops "pigs" would not pass formal vetting. I said I would not delete them. She said to lock my social media accounts until after vetting and that I could do what I wanted with them once I passed. I complied. I passed. I asked her why she liked me, why she wanted to hire me, though I was so outside the norm. She said she saw something in me that told her I'd go far. She said she liked my conviction. She said the governor believed that poetry was the missing link that would close the gap between his legacy and the legacy of his father, a man known for his poetic speeches, speeches he had written himself. She said that Cuomo wanted his own Maya Angelou.

That statement sticks like putty to my consciousness now, with the question of why she liked me even more pressing than when I first asked it. The lead counsel was a brilliant but curmudgeonly woman who liked no one and had a lack of patience that you could hear from down the hall when she was berating someone. Only the governor was safe from her rampages, but she liked me. Why *did* she like me? Is it because she saw my waffling contradictions, my moral anxiety, my desperation to be accepted? Is it because she knew that I could be worn down and redesigned into a machine that fit her use?

Cuomo used only one of my speeches during the time I worked as his speechwriter. The poetics were too advanced, I like to think, for his mouth. I left speechwriting when I realized that I wasn't learning anything, that I wasn't gaining any useful experience, that I was just sitting there picking up a check. Then I moved into the press shop, where it was typical for me to spend time with the governor during press gaggles, a moment when, at the end of an event, press can ask any question, whether related to the event or not. On one such day, a reporter asked a question about Eric Garner. As is typical of a young communications staffer, my job was to clip every media mention of the governor, which meant that every mention of the governor that day included a mention of Eric Garner. Most broadcast news stations who would mention Eric Garner in the newscast would also feature the video of his death—context setting, I guess. If nearly every mention of Governor Cuomo came with a mention of Eric Garner, then it meant I watched Eric Garner die nearly a hundred times. Almost every newscast that day replayed the gruesome iPhone-recorded transmission of Garner's murder, his breath growing thinner and thinner in the elbow grip of the police officer whose illegal (but what does it matter that the act is illegal if legality applies only to the populace but never to the system's watchmen?) choke hold slowly extinguishes the life of this father, this uncle, this man who planted trees.

I should say that it doesn't really matter that Eric Garner was a father, or an uncle, or a man who planted trees. His life was precious without association, without categorization, and I resent that I still feel the need to qualify it.

I watched him die on repeat, watched his family weep on repeat, watched community members mourn and rage on repeat, late into the afternoon. I was the only press staffer on clips that day, and the next morning. No one even thought to consider that this might be uniquely triggering for me, a Black woman of the Trayvon Martin generation. The next day, I was the only Black staffer in the communications office. Of nearly twelve people, there was just me. Usually, I went unseen, ignored, dismissed (except for the sweet head of speechwriting, who would sullenly shake his head as he watched me be passed over and unleveraged by the department). But that day, they asked me to take the first pen on a statement from the governor regarding Eric Garner.

I had learned, within the short scope of my expertise, that

the negotiation between writer and principal was a formally antagonistic one: The writer says, in the principal's voice, what the writer thinks the principal should say, and the writer pretends it was all the principal's idea—a subtle maneuver that, for just a moment, puts unprecedented power into the writer's hands.

I ran down to the office of my friend T, an older Black woman who had come to be my good friend and a mentor who worked in the administration.

"T, this is an opportunity, right?" I asked, nearly begging her to affirm me.

"Yes," she said, her voice flat with trepidation, "but be careful. You'll be the target. So be careful."

I ran to every other Black member of the administration that I had a relationship with. Most of them were heads-down, bootstraps kind of people whom I'd come to love through the math of isolation. They had come to love me too, though my youthful, "radical," impulsive, arrogant ambition and mercurial nature made them anxious. They worried that I had misunderstood my role, or that my insistence on transforming the role would present an incongruence that would eventually harm me, and perhaps them too. I went around to all of them, taking polls—*What should I say? What can I say we'll do?*

I went to the governor's chief counsel, a Black attorney who had graduated from the same law school as my mother. We had never spoken before this moment, though I had attempted to grab his attention many times. When we passed in the hallways, he would stride by with focused intent, my existence completely irrelevant to his purpose. I was not offended by it: I knew his type. Black only in a room of Black people, but otherwise uncategorizable, blank. I went to him because it was time, because even though he had avoided and ignored me, he was the only one with the authority and power to make it possible for the governor to do anything useful. He was quiet at first, leg folded over his knee, sitting back in the big chair that sat behind the grand mahogany desk that marked the size of the room. I could see his annoyance with me, could sense that he felt I was out of bounds.

I remember writing the statement as a poet would: thoughtful, careful, mission-driven. In my statement, the governor called for an end to the racist policing that makes Black communities feel unsafe. My boss, the head speechwriter, liked it; he thought it was smart, progressive, and useful. The statement never made it past the press secretary's desk. We did issue a statement that evening, and you could see a whisper of the version I'd written in the text that went out. I'd written the Garner statement poetically, and it was impressive. By the time it had been edited, that poetic framework was there, the tone of lament was there, but the intent had been changed, the language shifted just slightly to avoid accountability, to avoid calling out systemic racism, to avoid any acknowledgment of generations of complicity, and to avoid promising any kind of meaningful change. So it was no longer a statement but an empty lamentation.

That night, I would lie sleepless as Eric Garner's face flashed across my eyes, while through the governor, I assured the state of New York that I would "do something" about his death, a death about which I could do nothing, about which I had no power but that of the pen, the power to cosplay as a person with power, where the only power I did have was taken away in a

Google doc, where the few words that might have mattered were stricken from the record with callous considerations.*

That should have been enough, I agree. I'm sure you are wondering why I did not pick up and run at the sight of these obvious signifiers, at the start of this futile labor. I have no excuse but youth and the chiding fear that I would look in the mirror and see only a fraud if I chose to give up.

Not too long after, I became a press secretary, a coveted job in the press shop that would situate me within high-level press operations and ensure that I always had a job in the sector, ensure that I always had value to the political theater, allowing my talents to be reproduced toward the maintenance and protection of the very systems I scrutinized. A good government job. The irony was keeping me up at night. I came into the world of politics after the death of Trayvon Martin because living in my devastation didn't feel like enough. I felt I couldn't honestly say that I was fighting for change until I understood how change could happen within the constraints of political and legislative action. And there I was, in my good government job, a cog in the big wheel of boundless power, and all I could do was run through halls in the Kenneth Cole heels I could barely walk in, pretending that my proximity to power meant access to power. I was becoming an actor, building transferable skills that would shape my professional identity for the next decade. An identity that would benefit me and then betray me in more ways than one. I was a political operative with an ancient weapon at my

---

* For almost five years, the Justice Department hemmed and hawed over whether to bring federal civil rights charges against Daniel Pantaleo, the officer who choked Eric Garner to death.

disposal. They all wanted my poetry as long as it was devoid of my voice.* Then, one day before the fifth anniversary of Garner's death, Attorney General William Barr ordered that the case be dropped.

And to this day, not a single police officer involved in the death of Eric Garner has been held accountable for ending his life. Slowly, through coercion and immersion, I was becoming part of the structure's DNA.

---

* "What are the tyrannies you swallow day by day and attempt to make your own," Audre Lorde asks in "The Transformation of Silence into Language and Action," "until you will sicken and die of them, still in silence?" Paper delivered at the Modern Language Association's "Lesbian and Literature Panel," Chicago, Ill., December 28, 1977, first published in *Sinister Wisdom* 6 (Summer 1978) and *The Cancer Journals* (Spinsters Ink, 1980).

8.147 Executive Order No. 147: A Special Prosecutor to Investigate and Prosecute Matters Relating to the Deaths of Civilians Caused by Law Enforcement Officers

WHEREAS, ▓▓▓ the ▓▓▓
▓▓▓ laws ▓▓▓ are ▓▓▓ executed; ▓

NOW, THEREFORE, I, ▓▓▓
▓▓▓
▓▓▓
▓▓▓ hereby require ▓▓▓
▓▓▓
▓▓▓ the death of ▓
▓▓▓
▓▓▓
▓▓▓ Law ▓▓▓

FURTHER, for any matter ▓▓▓
▓▓▓
▓▓▓
▓▓▓
▓▓▓
▓▓▓ the ▓▓▓
▓▓▓
▓▓▓ term(s) ▓
▓▓▓
▓▓▓ will provide ▓▓▓
▓▓▓
▓▓▓ the ▓▓▓ return ▓

CHAPTER 6

THE SPIRITUAL

I spent the weeks after the 2020 general election manic and forlorn, drinking too much and licking my wounds in my Boston apartment with no job. I'd served on Elizabeth Warren's presidential campaign as director of strategic and surrogate communications for ten months, and we had lost. Biden, whom we were competing against, had won the primary and subsequent election. I had spent ten months contorting myself and my politics in order to participate in the process in a meaningful way. I of course believed that we should have done more and gone further left, but once again, I had fallen in line and gotten so little progress out of it. Disgusted with myself and frustrated with the question of whom I should be offering my labor to, I had nothing to do but read and try to get back to my own authentic poetic voice after another season of giving it. I read voraciously: Césaire and Jordan and Giovanni and Plato and Baldwin and Lorde and McKay and Moten. I would read and cry, my frustration and confusion manifesting in tearful breakdowns during which I would question everything I thought I knew about myself, everything I thought I knew about my life's work and ambition, running through the last year of my life in my head, analyzing each decision, each thought experiment. I was mourning the old me—the person who truly believed that poetry was enough to motivate voters and inspire new political futures.

In Elizabeth Warren's New Year's Eve speech during the campaign, of which I wrote a majority, I went for broke. Instead of a practical speech that reiterated campaign promises, this was a speech about imagination. When we were told that the speech would be delivered at Boston's Old South Meeting House, where the Boston Tea Party was organized and also where Phillis Wheatley, the first Black woman to publish poetry in the United States, was a member of the church, we knew that we had to honor her life as we pursued this idea of imagination, of a shared imagination that would change our world. This decision was in alignment with my then politics, which believed that poetry could be the convincing force that would save U.S. democracy.

"I want to tell you about one of the people who sat in this very room," I wrote.

> A young girl. A young, enslaved girl named Phillis Wheatley: Born in West Africa, Phillis was kidnapped by slave traders and brought to New England in 1761. From a young age it was clear that Phillis was an extraordinary person. She mas-

tered English, Latin, Greek, and English literature at a time when enslaved people could be condemned to death for learning. As she entered her teen years, she became a writer. Back in the early 1770s, as she sat in this church, in these pews, Phillis scoured the holy scripture for the words she needed to give voice to her visions and to spark her imagination.

She imagined a world that did not yet exist, but a world she could see. She penned ideals of a better America. Ultimately, she inspired leaders like George Washington himself. She showed through her work the power of imagination to help fuel a revolution.

Week after week, Phillis came to this room and imagined. Years before the Revolutionary War, she became the first Black woman to publish a book of poetry in America. Her imagination is woven into the tapestry of America's story.

So, just for a moment, here in this place of ideas that took root and shaped a nation, here on the eve of a New Year, let us come together to imagine. Imagine what our country will look like, imagine what your own life will look like, when we finally turn this page in our history.

What didn't make it into the speech was a reflection on the rest of Phillis Wheatley's story. While honored and lauded now, she was first disgraced when placed on trial by eighteen of Boston's elite men, which included persons such as Thomas Hutchinson, a colonial historian and governor of Massachusetts. She was being tried not because of any crime, but because these eighteen men felt that a Black woman could not have been talented enough to have written those poems. She was asked to defend her craft and prove that she was a poet to these eighteen men who likely lacked the fortitude or skill to be poets. Wheatley's imagination was so expansive, and so profound, that it was unimaginable to this class of wealthy white men that it could belong to her. What does that say about the value of the Black woman's voice, or her poetics? What does that say about the arbiters of democracy, who required that Phillis prove herself worthy of the literature that only she could make?

We were selling the idea of transformative imagination to a crowd of the political elite in the same church where Phillis Wheatley went to commune with her God. The same Phillis Wheatley who was penalized and interrogated for having an imagination at all. In retrospect, the speech feels so ill-fitting, so dishonest. This is to say nothing about the other collaborators of the speech or even Elizabeth Warren herself. This is to say that the prospect of having an imagination is already a contested and criminalized thing for those of us who do not belong to the ruling class.

In that speech, we asked the audience "to imagine a country where private prisons and detention centers don't exist and no one makes a profit from locking people up." We asked them "to imagine a country where no politician has to kiss the rings of the rich in order to win elected office." We asked them to imagine a country without corruption in Washington, a country where the gun industry does not target our children, a country that would be safe from climate change.

But what we didn't do was name who and what stood in the way of actualizing that imagined world. It was not just the Republican Party. It was not just Trump. It was not just Biden. It was the entire political ecosystem that gets in the way of these goals, that disrupts the possibility of these goals.

In that speech, my job was to write about and into the future. My job was to inspire people to work hard for change. My job was to get people to want the world that our campaign was selling. Just three months later, Elizabeth Warren dropped out of the race after a disappointing performance on Super Tuesday, finishing third in Massachusetts, her home state, which had already elected her senator. People didn't want the imagined world we were offering. It was unconvincing in the face of a fractured democracy that had room only for the old guard of the Democratic Party or the fascists of the Republican Party. There was no political imagination that could work within the confines of party politics. I had been convinced that the rhetorical tools of poetry could elevate Elizabeth Warren among people who needed desperately to be inspired.

The speech came from a good place. But ultimately it was a betrayal.

I'd spent nearly a decade fighting for Democratic values, slowly realizing that lowercase-d democracy was the crisis and that we were hostages to it, especially those of us who saw our own political efficacy within its framework.

By participating within the confines of the framework, by offering poetry up as a tool that could be used to help politicians make better rhetorical choices that might move people to vote, I became what I was fighting against. By attempting to become part of it in order to transform it, I betrayed myself. In both examples, I had made my body and mind completely available to the appeal of electoral politics, to attempt to understand the argument that had been made on its behalf. Each time, I failed. Each time, I used language as a tool, and it was thrown back at me.

This restless cyclicality is held up by what Frank B. Wilderson III calls the "default of the political," held up by the persistence of the colonizer's ethics as the centrifugal expression of its politics. I wanted to be an insurgent, but I could be no more than an aide. "Thank you," Elizabeth Warren wrote to me in a note of appreciation for my work on the campaign, "for the poetry you brought to everything you did. I'm grateful."

I realized then, as I sat in my Boston apartment, that part of what had changed was my relationship to poetry. I had not sat down and read—really read—a poem since before the campaign. Throughout the campaign, I approached all poetic texts with an extractive impulse; I was pulling poetic texts to see what I could borrow from them that would help me write better speeches. It occurred to me that part of why I was so sad was that I was empty. My creative well had been drained. I had lost all connection to the apparatus that makes me feel, that really moves me. When I sat down to think about what I'd need to save myself from that terrifying post-campaign depression, it was poetry that called out to me. I needed poetry to affirm and comfort me.

Audre Lorde, in her famed 1977 essay "Poetry Is Not a Luxury," declares that poetry is a revolutionary act. An act—not an occupation or a belonging but requirement for the writer and the reader to *do* something. Poetry is a system of lines in a triangulated graph that helps us analyze and comprehend our various subjectivities, that helps us identify oppressive structures, that helps us to liberate and defend. Poetry, Lorde says, "is the skeleton architecture of our lives," in which the foundations of change ask us to walk toward the bridge of our fears, where on the other side exists a world that "has never been before." For Lorde, poetry is not simply a rhetorical tool but a gesture that has the power to illuminate human connectivity and inspire the practice of imagination. I needed to start building the lexicon of resistance, to start thinking about poetry as an act instead of a tool, and this essay gave me the direction I had labored to find.

In these months, I would lie submerged in a tub or starfished in bed and listen to June Jordan read "Poem About My Rights."* If you've heard it, then you know it is impossible not to end up crying, to end up holding your knees in fetal position, feeling the air fold in on you in a different way than it ever had before. Then you know that this poem is an education (if one agrees that an education is simply an ambition that creates pathways toward other learnings).

"Poem About My Rights" begins by continuing. "Even tonight, and I need to take a walk..." The line begins with "even," letting us know that this thought, this thinking, has come from somewhere, though we know nothing about where or from how long ago. The poem then goes on to do the work of continuing by establishing presence, with Jordan confirming that she has a body (which she tells us in the same breath with which she reveals her body's need to take a walk) so that she can

---

* June Jordan, *Passion: New Poems, 1977–1980* (Beacon Press, 1980).

deal with this poem, clear her head about it, but the impulse to take a walk is confronted by this greater condition, the one that surrounds her like the night, the one that forces her to question "why I can't go out without changing my clothes my shoes / my body posture my gender identity . . ."

The question almost instantly answers itself through the logics of negation—"because I am the wrong / sex the wrong age the wrong skin"—and Jordan takes a moment to travel, to enter a world of her choice, where she can think, really think, about the big ideas, but is once again disrupted from thinking by the reality of this body and of the social limitations placed on it. And then Jordan questions the violent French suggestion that "if the guy penetrates but does not ejaculate then he did not rape me" by wondering how much force and defense she would have had to show to make it clear that a woman did not consent, but knowing that there would be no threshold where her lack of consent would be valued in her society, it then becomes a metaphor about the social violence in South Africa "penetrating into Namibia" and Angola, an image that tells us all we need to know about the directional mobility of colonization: that it leverages the penetrating violence it deploys on one community toward the penetrating violence it will deploy on another community, leveraging money, resources, and bodies toward the destruction of each.

Then she wonders, even if her body were to resist, and the movements of Zimbabwe and Angola and Namibia were to resist (which they did), and lose, would the "big boys" claim that there was consent? Would they say that Zimbabwe and Angola and Namibia were responsible for their own colonization? To which the answer is, yes, of course—a reminder that the winner steals the rights to the stories of history. Now that she has gone macro, she stays there for a minute, out in the world outside her body, notably, with one small step followed by a bigger one, an iambic foot. She name-checks the CIA and their murders of Kwame Nkrumah and Patrice Lumumba, but then she closes the scope again, focusing on her father, who was killed, at least metaphorically, by the CIA's subtle attack on the Black consciousness, by which it convinced people like her father that they were wrong and did not belong in the same institutions of whiteness because "he was wrong the wrong age the wrong skin," a mythology that she knows shares the same logic as the patriarchy and sexism that led her father to want a boy instead of June. She concludes by giving the body a break from the narratives of its circumstance, by declaring *"I am not wrong: Wrong is not my name,"* and then returns the agency of the body to itself by giving it the right and the expectation of self-defense, the right and expectation of self-determination, which "may very well cost you your life," a generous threat that sets the boundary around the body, making it clear that self-preservation is the ultimate concern of the body now that it knows and has released all that it knows about the relationships between gender violence, patriarchy, and imperialism.

And you cannot not cry on your first encounter with this poem because, by the end of it, you now know these things too, if you hadn't already, that these sociopolitical power structures intersect both in their construction and in their impact. You cannot not cry because, if you are a person who is not a cis heterosexual man, you already knew this even if you'd never had the language to articulate it—that the same forces working to displace the people from their lands, that the same capitalism that makes it impossible for you to pursue a healthy, joyous life, is conspiring with colonialism and patriarchy and heteronormativity and every oppressive structure that relies on your oppression to keep you from thinking with your full capacity, as it does to June, as it does to all of us, to keep us from organizing against it.

"Poem About My Rights" asked me, "Do you know your own name?" And I had to respond by going back to my books in order to redefine myself. During that time in Boston, I needed to remember that my relationship to poetry was a dialogue.

I wept when I listened to June Jordan's poem because I realized how tired my body was, how I had exhausted myself by trying to answer all of these big questions alone, by flattening my politics into a liberal praxis, which I did because it was easier to understand and explain, easier than writing this book. I wept because I knew I had not been thinking as hard and as critically as I could have been thinking.

June Jordan's poetry has, without sacrificing beauty, music, or craft, helped bring us back into our bodies, helped us name what we feel. This is what all poetry has the capacity to do.

Though "Poem About My Rights" is not technically a call-and-response poem, it proves that in many ways, every poem is a call-and-response poem. The call-and-response poem is one of the oldest forms of poetry, the titular form in which the poem calls to the listener and the listener responds. Every poem we read calls out to us, and whether somatically or intellectually, we do respond, even if it is to turn away. The call-and-response is a template. In fact, all art can be understood within the principles of call-and-response. Also known as antiphony, call-and-response is an aspect of African American oral tradition, a tradition carried over Atlantic waters from native African lands. Oral traditions, particularly call-and-response, are interactive performances, and a fundamental condition of communication. To respond, you must be called to, directed to, gestured to. The antiphony signifies, the antiphony engages with its legacy, the antiphony is intertextual and intergenerational, the antiphony is cooperation, the antiphony is humanness distilled.

Enslaved Black people laboring in fields and plantations across the U.S., Canada, and the Caribbean used call-and-response in spirituals and in what the poet Yusef Komunyakaa called Sorrow Songs. These were not just songs that expressed despair, they were songs that allowed folks to check on and in with one another, and allowed them to organize rebellion covertly. I can feel the textures of call-and-response when standing in the middle of a protest: "What do we want?" "Justice!" "When do we want it?" "Now!" That interaction requires community, requires being followed and being led. Call-and-response is the study of Black struggle and resistance, a study undergone in the Black church, in Black defiance, in Black remembrance. These calls are hymns, and their responses fill the hymn with urgency, with the now. This lineage is one of honor, is one of critical necessity, is a performance of discourse, of confession. The call needs a response, and is not ashamed to say so.

To understand call-and-response, we must also understand it in poetic lineage. Call-and-response is a tradition that prioritizes interaction between two elements, be they human or nonhuman. It comes from a people who understood that language, both verbal and nonverbal, is meant to usher a reaction, meant to elicit a response. Emerging from the folktales, chants, and rituals of our ancestry, call-and-response comes naturally to the Black poet. It is built into us, the idea that the subject must interact with the world outside it to receive what it is calling for. The Black poet reproduces this relationship in the material of our gifts, we reproduce this relationship in our methodology:

> God is good!
> All the time.

Words mean things. And meanings change over time. It is the poem that reminds us about where they came from, and about what we've lost (or gained) in leaving them behind. When themes written in 1956, like the line "Seven at the Golden Shovel" in Gwendolyn Brooks's "We Real Cool," show up in 2015, as in Terrance Hayes's poem "The Golden Shovel," we know that time is an active, living thing.[*] We know that the call has been passed down generationally and that the response is in us all, waiting to be repurposed, waiting to be reintroduced.

The poem calls, and with our bodies we respond—with tears, with the fine hair of the skin standing on end, with a deep breath, with a thought that engages the thought that sparked it. In this cycle of intuitive call-and-response, the poem activates the ancestral relationship between human and language. This relationship is replicated in every poem, every piece of art, every part of how we relate to one another. In that logic, it follows that the poem is the most complete (and still complex) example of this rhetorical phenomenon.

---

[*] Gwendolyn Brooks, *The Bean Eaters* (Harper, 1960); Terrance Hayes, *Lighthead: Poems* (Penguin Books, 2010).

The challenge is to let the poem speak to you, to let it call to you, and in response, allow it to radicalize you. To allow it to change you. To allow it to transform your idea of humanity, to transform your understanding of human interconnectivity. To let it be the start of a long conversation with the world around you, this world you are constantly responding to, this world that is calling to and responding back to you. This oral tradition, this conversation, transcends time so that we are always calling on history and responding with the present. Being in conversation with the past is what gets us closer to a collective understanding, is what gets us closer to knowing what the devil is wearing, to knowing what rock the devil is likely to crawl out from under. The call and the response are where we begin, as people, as thinkers, as poets. The body calls and the body responds. The legal and political structures of power assume parentage over all of our bodies via the logic of patriarchy, taking away our sovereign relationships to mind and body, intercepting the body's call with another prescriptive response.

When we kneel at the threshold of the body, listen to its call and understand the response we owe to it, we begin to understand justice. The body calls, but the law does not respond to the body's call. The paternal state will not listen when we, its subjects, attempt to tell them what our bodies are telling us about need and rights. When we are cold and sick and hungry and tired, it is our bodies that tell us what the power structures pretend not to know: Housing is a human right, healthcare is a human right, access to healthful food is a human right. The law responds to the needs and desires of the powerful.

Our society thinks of the body as a weapon, as a tool of the racial capitalist dynamic that forces us into production and reproduction. It eliminates the conversation between the body and its ecosystem as it renders some bodies more valid than others.

Poetry is neutral. It does not care or *not* care, it simply has concerns. It is concerned with music and language and how they form in the mouth. But because it is responsive, it can offer the language of care if care is what the writer intends and care is what the reader receives. I began to write poems about care, about love, about the questions I was asking myself about political effectualization and ideology.

We rely on poems that testify and reify and remind. But the poem can never be pure. It is not the poem that changes the world, but the poem that changes the person. I became a different person in that apartment, a person who knew that she had to become a different person in order to make space for the truth, a person who was willing to ask questions that went against everything I thought I already knew.

DO YOU BELIEVE IN BORDERS?

Camonghne Felix

What I am feeling   is the death   of a million
wayward bodies   falling into each other

like lattice work   on a French pie
I draw   a river   and your god   lines it out into a field

I say this earnestly   and with a smile   so I'm not sure
what   you're asking   me is it a question of shoulds   or

of ares   the nation state   is a body   it is the Russian doll
of bodies   a body housing   a body of   farmed bodies

all of whom   mill about in their   categorical nothingness
with some parasite   sucking from   their breast

all over   the globe
one breast   drains into the mouth   of a whole class

A safety   valve   for the gutless
You have to   understand   my parameters here

are limited, The space   between   my two selves
shrinking and   pulverized   all the same.

The wine delivery   comes   My courier   steps
into the foyer   I say hello   I say   thank you   I   sign

her   receipt   I   offer her   a Clorox   wipe
I stand away   at six feet. I   don't know.

I do know   Nobody   dies
at my   border.

—October 8, 2020

CHAPTER 7

THE POLITICS OF NOW

In 2020, months into the COVID-19 crisis, I left Boston and moved to Washington, D.C., where I would start to turn back to the beginning. I scrolled the internet for ways to reconnect, looked for mutual aid opportunities, tried to join D.C.'s DSA, failed to stay consistent. It felt hard to show up, it felt hard to be honest about the fact that I had not shown up since I had stepped into the electoral world, and it felt embarrassing to admit that I had been absent because I lost faith and fell into the presumption that change could happen only if all efforts were focused on driving people to the polls to elect incrementalists without the conviction to actually fight for their constituents' dignity. In the fifteenth and sixteenth centuries, as more and more enslaved Africans were brought to the Caribbean and Brazil, maroon communities of enslaved Africans were formed, with enslaved people running into the hills to form their own free societies in parts of land their slavers were too afraid to venture into, deeming them to be unlivable. The marooners stole from their former slavers, created their own culture, raised their families outside the plantation, outside the prison. These "runaways" and their radical rebellion are where imagination met materiality. This tradition of escape, of living a life outside the conditions and constraints decided on your behalf, is buried in me.

What can be made in the shadow of democracy when capitalism, imperialism, and colonization are assumed to be the righteous principles of democracy? What can be made in the shadow of capitalism when capitalism creates the conditions that form any state? I was wrestling with the question, first asked by the theorist and organizer Eric A. Stanley in his book *Atmospheres of Violence* (2021): "Are we in a broken democracy or a functionally democratic society that betrays the potential true democracy may possess?"*

In D.C., I needed to find a job, so with the support of a mentor I launched a new communications practice geared toward left and progressive candidates who needed people who really understood the role of communication in a political campaign and what it meant to motivate people. I took this job with the intention to leverage some of what I'd learned on the Warren campaign to help progressive and leftist candidates like Tiffany Cabán and Jamaal Bowman in New York City, who were better than the candidates I'd worked with before and actually

---

* Eric A. Stanley, *Atmospheres of Violence: Structuring Antagonism and the Trans/Queer Ungovernable* (Duke University Press, 2021).

had visions for the future that I could get behind. Even though I was doing good work, disillusionment had already gripped me and couldn't be shaken. I knew that even when we were winning, we were losing.

During the 2022 midterm elections, each campaign I worked on was a reminder of my own futility. I tried to get my clients to lean into radical honesty, to, for instance, reject a two-state solution for Palestine; to, at the very least, support BDS—boycott, divestment, and sanctions against Israel—and vote no on pro-Israel legislation. In 2020, a Pew report showed that most young people wanted the Democratic Party to lean away from Israel and toward Palestine.* One of my clients was running in a progressive district where data showed that half the voters felt concerned about the occupation; I wasn't working from my gut only. Even though this was a popular position, our decision to run on a pro-BDS and pro-Palestine platform was met with a campaign of attacks that chipped away at our numbers every day. The opposing candidate went as far as to call my client antisemitic because she brought Pepsi and challah to dinner with a rabbi. These attacks were relentless, and against my recommendations, my client walked back her position and downplayed her commitment to BDS.

Before this, we were tied for first place. The other candidate had a huge war chest—he even donated $4 million of his own money to his campaign†—and AIPAC, the Israel lobby, pumped

---

* Laura Silver, "Younger Americans Stand Out in Their Views of the Israel-Hamas War," Pew Research Center, April 2, 2024.

† Jeff Coltin, "The Congressional Candidates Donating the Most Money to Their Own Campaigns," *City & State*, August 19, 2022.

hundreds of thousands of dollars into a stealth PAC that supported him and targeted us, which included spending more than $400,000 on mailers that characterized my client's support for BDS as antisemitic.* Our opponent was running as a centrist and using centrist talking points—early in the race, in the wake of *Roe*'s overturn, he said he would "not object" to restrictions on abortion, which he later walked back when his campaign realized that this would have been a dealbreaker for that progressive district. The race was rigged even before he entered. The Democrat-led New York State legislature had gerrymandered the map, shifting the boundaries of New York districts, in an effort to get the advantage in twenty-two of the twenty-six districts. This meant that progressive candidates were shoved into new and congested districts, creating chaos on the map and ultimately forcing candidates with almost identical platforms to run against each other and split progressive votes. Mondaire Jones, for instance, who was then considered a progressive and was allied with my candidate, moved out of his district in the Lower Hudson Valley and Rockland County to my candidate's district, in an unbelievable betrayal. All of this made the possibility that Republicans would control the House of Representatives much higher. The end result was a laughable failure. Eleven New York congressional districts would elect Republicans, many more than the Democrats expected after projecting that only four districts would vote Republican.

With the cards stacked against us, we still managed to come in second, which somehow feels worse than coming in last. Our

---

* Michael Arria, "AIPAC Says It Helped Defeat NY-10 Candidate over Her BDS Stance," *Mondoweiss,* August 24, 2022.

opponent received only 26 percent of the progressive vote out of 38,142 progressive voters—but beat us by 1,300 votes. We were so close, and we lost because of a political landscape that disenfranchised us from the beginning.

A week after the midterms, Donald Trump announced his candidacy for president, no doubt ignited by the success of the Supreme Court in overturning *Roe*. As I watched this maniacal demagogue once again enter the race for leadership of the country, I couldn't help but laugh at the irony of *Roe* going down right before he decided to return. It was obvious that this would happen, written in the stars.

During his presidency, President Obama had eight years to work with Congress to codify *Roe v. Wade* into federal law. He campaigned on signing the Freedom of Choice Act and told the Planned Parenthood Action Fund in 2008 that it would be the first thing he'd do as president. Yet even in 2009, he told a CNN reporter that codifying *Roe* was "not of the highest legislative priority." President Obama and the Democrats chose not to do so despite the Democrats' total control of Congress during the four-month window in 2008 when the Affordable Care Act was passed in the Senate. Democrats took *Roe* off the table because of the potential political risks, because it was a barter, because in order to continue crossing the aisle, they knew they couldn't both pass Obamacare and codify the right to abortion into federal law. It was the single point in time, a small portal, when *Roe* could have passed without the risk of Republican dissent getting in the way. The Democrats did not use this moment to protect the lives of some of the most vulnerable people in the country—nonwhite people with uteruses who will suffer if they lose the right to a safe abortion—but used it as bait to keep a certain percentage of Democratic voters from questioning their allegiance to the Democratic Party, dangling the relief of a codified *Roe v. Wade* in front of us during every campaign season, yet letting voters down every year.

This is not just a matter of political baseball. As the Democrats plot short-term, incremental wins, they fail to leverage foresight toward long-term accomplishments that deliver lasting protections to working-class people who rely on these protections to stay alive. That failure opens up a small space for Republicans to stretch, little by little, until the space becomes a door and the door grows a threshold and over that threshold walks a figure like Donald Trump who has no loyalty to the Democrats' idea of democracy but owes full loyalty to capitalism, making him an alluring choice for any swing voter who is glad to see his kind of chaotic disruption happen in their name. This tendency to overpromise and underdeliver continues to be the Achilles' heel of the party, and almost all of the candidates we elect, no matter how radical they seem at first, capitulate to this brand of politics, this slow and clumsy work of doing the least in order to protect the idea of more.

And while there is no doubt that the Affordable Care Act was a cosmetic restructuring of the U.S. healthcare system, and the closest we've gotten to universal healthcare, it was still a capitalist endeavor that continues to turn a profit for insurance companies.

Joe Biden campaigned on a promise to codify *Roe v. Wade* into law in 2020 and again in 2024. He repeated this promise during his 2024 State of the Union address as he made his case for reelection. Even though his ability to pass FOCA was much lower than President Obama's, he campaigned on this promise, assuring the country that *this time* he would get it done—without acknowledging how the mistakes of the last two decades, including that of the last year of Biden's presidency, make it even harder to get it done. As my friend Natasha Lennard says in her article "The End of *Roe:* Saving Abortion Rights Means Taking Them Into Our Own Hands," "It should never have come to this—the end of *Roe* with zero nationwide legislative protections for abortion access."*

Where the Democratic Party fails to protect abortion for those already living in a post-*Roe* world due to draconian state laws, community steps in, and this was true before the fall of *Roe*. Abortion funds across the country exist within a wide network of grassroots organizations dedicated to building power to counter the financial and political barriers to safe abortion care. These orgs, often run by Black and Brown organizers, already knew that safe abortion access is under threat every day—and they know not to rely on Democratic leadership in their fight.

Party allegiance prevents us from seeing clearly the ways we have been let down. It muddies our visions of solidarity. We are all subject to the games of a system that gives us no chance to write the rules.

Roe is one example, but there are many others that highlight the contradictions of the party. The Democrats fail to correct the errors of the past and struggle to learn from the needs of the

---

* Natasha Lennard, "The End of Roe: Saving Abortion Rights Means Taking Them Into Our Own Hands," *The Intercept,* May 3, 2022.

present. The Democrats have underestimated the public's readiness to confront the party. But, much like the relationship between poet and reader, the poem works only when it is in conversation, when it responds to the reader's assumptions and anxieties, when it creates a bridge between the eye and the page. The poem evolves to meet the needs of the reader. The poem then becomes the need of the reader when the reader finds herself considered in or by the poem. The Democrats continue to fail because they respond to corporate interests. The Democrats continue to fail because they fail to respond to the voter. The voter is not a corporation. There's a list of antagonisms that drive the Democratic voter away from the party, including the overwhelming reality of big money in politics.

Once Trump returned as a possibility, I felt a sense of obligation. What was I supposed to do but lend my labor to the progressive agenda? How would I explain what I was doing at that time, who I was doing it for? What would I tell the next generation about this moment and my contribution to beating back the force that would spiral us into the end of it all? Unlike previous years, I was blanking on how to effectively beat back the overwhelmingly Republican-Trumpian messaging that had captured parts of the country.

Trump's messaging did everything that you would expect from a right-wing populist—he ran on a nationalist agenda that spoke to people's fears, an agenda that would appeal to those who feel disempowered, even if that is not inherently true: "This will not be my campaign. This will be our campaign."

Trump is smart enough to understand that people are vulnerable to a poetics that makes them feel they are the winners, that they are the victors, especially at the expense of those who feel as though others' safety is in conflict with theirs. I imagine that this is how the peasants of Portugal felt when the language of the papal bull *Romanus Pontifex* of 1455 was sold to them: that they could become part of the ruling class if others became the peasants, if others became the slaves.

"There has never been anything like it," he says to his followers, "this great movement of ours. Never been anything like it, and perhaps there will never be anything like it again."

Trump represents a turning tide, the rise of fascism in a world that was unprepared to resist it. The various tendencies of our politico-economic reality—the tendencies that tell us how fascism approaches its potential—went untended to as the world watched governments in many countries move further right. After all this time, from Mussolini to Hitler, the establishment failed to see someone like Trump being elevated to the highest office in the land. A series of oversights and badly formed strategies defined the opportunity for someone like Trump to gain a foothold.

The Democratic Party, besieged with their fear of the return of Trump, forgot to campaign on hope. We descend into fascism with little defense. What's left to counter the tide of fascism is the growing tide of community. Of mutual and reciprocal responsibility. They forgot to campaign on the result of our disillusionment, which was a confrontation with the evilest energies of our world, and a confrontation with the most passive and actively violent realities of what a modern-day democracy is.

Trump is a stand-alone demagogue. He is also a symptom of, and reflection of, a broken democracy. He was not born in a vacuum. Trump is the manifestation of Republican extremism and Democratic passivity. Trump is the manifestation of the U.S. anti-Black political legacy that made it possible for him to lose the popular vote in 2016 but win the election. The rise of technocratic oligarchs like Jeff Bezos and Elon Musk is a result of the anti-working-class policies and approaches that have centered the needs of corporations and the one percent for decades.

As I watched the electoral race shape up, I realized just how terrible a candidate Joe Biden was. His team had no original messaging; it ran simply on an anti-Trump platform, on anti-Trump fear, which worked—as it was designed to do—to corner people in their fear, to exploit it. I also felt trapped into this corner. What else was there to feel but fear? There was no reason to feel optimistic, there was no reason to feel we were moving forward; all we knew was that we were afraid of moving back.

At the turn of each election cycle, we are asked to accept small compromises as wins, and are expected to have endless patience for the lethargic nature of government. We are asked to wait, cycle after cycle, for the change we are promised, and all the while, our elected officials never stop campaigning. They fail us day after day and knock on our doors at 7 P.M., when the children are sleepy and hungry, when dinner is already an hour late, to ask us if we still plan to vote for their candidate, the candidate who had been elected twelve months ago and has done nothing more than install a streetlight. We vote insincerely because we are told we must be strategic with our power.

All this strategy, decades of strategy, and we still ended up with Donald Trump. One Democratic candidate on the 2016 stage (whom we made exceptions for, whom we voted "strategically" for), and we still ended up with Donald Trump. Eight Democratic candidates on the 2020 stage—and we still ended up with Donald Trump four years later.

The operations of the electoral system rely on political theater and ritual to perform equality, to convince us that we are active participants in the decision-making of democracy, and in the mitigations and litigations of democracy. But we are ultimately the subjects of an electoralism that compromises democracy's supposed qualities. Fred Moten tells us that this counterinsurgent subversion is the point.

U.S. democratic politics is a mode of crisis management whose most conspicuous and extravagant rituals—elections and inaugural celebrations and protests—operate at the level of the demonstration. Elections in the United States are meant, finally and above all, to demonstrate that an election took place—a central consideration for structures of authority that depend on the eclipse of democratic content by the ritual animation of supposedly democratic forms.... The United States is the land of formal democratic enclosure.*

I was exhausted with dumping my energy into a black hole of "strategy." It just wasn't working. I wondered if it was all my fault, wondered if I had the talents I had been hired over and over again to exploit. I felt I didn't belong. Here I was, trying to reconcile the moment, thinking really hard about it, while my

---

* Fred Moten, *Democracy: Keywords for American Cultural Studies* (NYU Press, 2014).

friends and colleagues fell into the hyperfocus on Trump. As the pandemic raged on, all I could think about was how many people were dying alone in their homes, wishing that someone had checked in on them. People needed food. Elders needed medicine. Children needed their education. What were any of us doing? What change were we making? We were moving voters, sure, but to where?

As I phased out of this work, these questions were the ones on my mind. Whenever I spoke to press or did television interviews, I made sure to bring everything back to the need for Democrats to actually deliver messaging that would show people that they were actively solving the problems killing us, not just waxing eloquent about them as leverage for the votes. I made sure to always bring things back to how vulnerable the Democrats were leaving us with toothless strategies that failed to operate outside the scope of fear. It just wasn't enough to move me, and I imagine that for a lot of people, it wasn't enough to move them either. The question was not only whether Democratic voters would vote Republican. The question was whether Democratic voters were going to show up at all. That required a motivating message. That required a policy-centric message. And in a world of fear and party loyalty, these questions were antagonistic and antidemocratic. It was clear after some time that I was so unaligned with the world I'd been working in that it was costing me friendships, respect. Of course it bothered me, because it isolated me. Few people around me wanted to ask these questions. Few people around me wanted to ask any real questions at all.

I made my way back to organizing because I needed a home. Because I needed to belong to people who understood the logic of interconnectedness, who would stand by that logic regardless of what carrot was dangled in front of their eyes. I came back to organizing because I'd exhausted my capacity to see, because I had spent almost a decade trying to fit my imagination into the frameworks that electoralism allowed for, almost a decade trying to suppress my impulse to "do my job."

I'd begun to deprogram myself, and I ached with conflict. It's not that I did not question power—I'd spent my whole life trying to answer questions of power, questions of who has it, who doesn't, and who needs to give it away—but deprogramming meant changing those questions. The questions now are, What is power? And how am I supposed to use it?

What I had in my hands was material, political power. There are politicians who would pick up on the first call when I rang, Very Powerful People who would call me in the middle of the night to know what I thought, to know what I thought about what they thought. And I promise you, fingers crossed, that on each call, even then, I fought for our representatives to do and say what was right, even when it was not expedient.

I fought to represent candidates that moderates call the far left, I fought for them to campaign on honesty, I fought for them to be their authentic selves, to focus on what they could change locally while keeping an eye on the federal landscape to fight against the tides that could make things worse for all of us. I wrote honest speeches, what I wrote was the truth, as close as I could get to it. And, often, I lost.

I told the candidates I worked with at the time to speak out on Israeli occupation, and that was a strike. I told them to call out white supremacy on the trail, and that was a strike. I told them to step away from Good Capitalism rhetoric. That was another strike. Every race, I felt I was failing, even when we were winning.

I couldn't break the binary. I couldn't tell my candidates to tell the truth and keep them in the game at the same time. So I took the job of the umpire and called myself *out!* I quit.

I began writing this book at the top of the pandemic and realized, as I was moving away from electoral politics, that the book I wanted to write was not about how politicians could use poetry to write better speeches, it was about how political rhetoric borrows from poetry's nature in order to distract us from the fight and convince us that power can only be owned by those who conquer.

I had power. But it wasn't real.

It was while organizing for Palestine that I realized what power really is. It's an avenue of resistance. Watching the world rise up against institutions that aid and abet genocide—including cultural behemoths and media monopolies that profit from genocide—is proof of our ability to see a different world for ourselves, to see a different world for our communities, to dream up a different language that writes a poem of our design. Palestine is a litmus test, as Angela Davis has said. Because it is a measure of how much you are willing to fight for life. As we moved into early 2024, I found myself immersed in this work, falling further and further into a productive rage, a rage that allowed me to better recognize the incongruities of that moment, and the kinds of interventions that were necessary to meet it.

I found myself most conflicted about the question of the vote. Should we vote? Some communists say no, many socialists say yes. All agree that the vote is as much a tool as it is a weapon that can be deployed or withheld in the service of change. Those of us who believe that voting is an important part of their work to organize their communities should vote and do whatever groundwork is required to shuttle those votes toward candidates most likely to advance our most radical idea of justice.

I struggle with those who believe that the vote is owed, and that the history of voter suppression is reason enough to consider it a compulsory responsibility. While my thoughts on this question shift across the spectrum from year to year, I still think that the vote should never be considered owed, because of these legacies of repression, because of these legacies of erasure. If the vote is understood as our only pathway to change, then all the other pathways shut down. The suggestion that the vote is the only way to participate in democracy (if your goal is to participate) is an intentionally compromising suggestion meant to guilt marginalized people into voting for a party that nominally represents their ideals but often fails to deliver. How many votes must it take to desegregate our schools? How many votes must it take to get healthful foods into our communities? How many votes must it take to redesign the relationship between landlord and tenant? The question then might also be, How many votes must be withheld before the party of the people realizes this need and takes critical, sweeping action to meet those demands? How many votes must be withheld before a new party emerges, a party interested in meeting the demands of the majority and resisting the pressure of the corporate minority? There must be space in our movements for the protest voter, the skeptical voter, the nonvoter.

When I told Kiese that we had only one option, that the vote was the only way, I was saying that we could challenge power only on its terms. I was working from the assumption that power is real only if it can be quantified, if it can be counted with a vote. There are the options we are given, and then there are the possibilities we forge when we decide to push beyond binaries and fight for what feels impossible, with no concessions. The poem concedes only to itself.

Language is political and historical praxis. From the papal bulls of Portugal to the slave codes of Georgia, these documents that shaped humanity's course show us that the language of history and the language of now have an effect on the way we learn to imagine. We are not simply in the fight to change the ethics of politicians, but in the fight to change the entire landscape of power. We begin to nurture an evolved ethics and morals and poetics that inspire working people to push to challenge that landscape with a true populist message, a message that allows us all to question our relationships to justice and freedom. The law begins to approach validity only when it speaks to the needs and calls of the people, a thing it can do only under the insistence and resilience of resistance.

Biden's second run for president felt like watching a bird fly into a window again and again and again. I can't count how many times I cringed at the gaffes, at the garbled speeches, at the stumbling press interviews. It felt as if we were watching, in real time, decades of failed Democratic strategy haunting the campaign. For example, the party had, yet again, locked up the field: Biden was considered the best option, with no serious consideration of other viable candidates. The party had, yet again, moved further to the right on key issues like immigration and failed to build a working coalition with working-class people.

When the party abruptly decided to take Joe Biden out of the race and pivoted to making Kamala Harris the party's nominee, it felt like a setup. How was a Black woman going to run a campaign in the shadow of the president who defined the party? Like Biden, she ran on a Trump-first campaign. Like Biden, she ran on a campaign that proposed the status quo. Like Biden, she continued to glorify Israel and erase Palestine in the face of hundreds of thousands of the horrific deaths that even the U.N., an incredibly flawed institution, had already called a genocide.

The 2024 Democratic National Convention showed the cognitive dissonance that drives the party. The convention's tagline is *Our future is created here* . . . but how can the party take us into the future when its platform belongs to the past?

Ahead of the 2024 election, we faced two problems: the re-election of Donald Trump and the election of Vice President Kamala Harris. Donald Trump is both diabolical and dangerous to the safety, welfare, and well-being of Americans and any subjects of colonial states worldwide.

But I also felt that there would be little to look forward to under a Harris presidency. Vice President Harris could very well have been a deeply affected insurgent who planned to infiltrate the Oval Office, but the Oval requires that she do the ugly work of maintaining the empire in order to be leader of the "free world." She would avoid many populist policies, not only to maintain leverage, but to maintain the favor of big money, even though the country is yearning for more populist policies. As the first Black and Brown woman president, she would also become an example of how democracy weaponizes identity to *flatten* identity. The fact of her marginalization would become a defense of her actions, even when they were immoral, as was already true when she was asked about Palestine or immigration. Instead of being evaluated critically by how she could move the country toward more radical ideals, she would be excused by the curse of low expectations. Because she is a Black woman, we would make exceptions that we should not make. We would say that she *had to* move further right in order to do the job, not realizing that this would constitute our submitting to what we all know is true.

Kamala, a tough-on-crime former state attorney who, for instance, willingly criminalized Black and Brown parents and children over truancy, would have been required to mirror the policies and actions of her predecessors, perhaps with the smallest amount of flexibility that would allow her to move just a tiny, tiny bit left. She would necessarily be a warmongering, tough-on-crime capitalist president. She would be, as she already is, a darling of the neoliberal project, and a deputy of the U.S. carceral project that shapes all of our systems, including our immigration policy. As a Black woman, it did not inspire me that Kamala Harris could rise to the top job in our country. It frightened me. Is this what will be expected of me next? Is this the kind of excellence I will be expected to aspire to? Black women have always been among the primary victims of white supremacy and state violence. Now we would be expected to prove our value to a capitalist economy that requires our labor to survive. We would be expected to get in line, to follow suit.

If she had won, we'd have had to watch Kamala Harris fit snugly into the template offered to her. We would have watched her be dehumanized by the template. We would have watched her be implicated by the template. She would have been scapegoated by the template. The inherent failures of the state would have become her failures. And because she is a brilliant Black woman, she would have become a representative of a post-racial society and she would have been held accountable to it more fiercely than anyone who came before her. This is the violence that Black women know all too well: the violence of perception, which suggests that a Black woman holding the highest position in the world would have been taken to mean that all Black women now had similar power. We could have expected everyday backlash from people who feel threatened by the idea of Black women having power.

Jamaal Bowman, whom I supported in the 2020 congressional elections, won that race mainly because he focused on meeting his voters where he could best access them: education. As a former teacher and principal, he brought expansive and unique thinking about how education could work for the district, a kind of thinking that the district had never seen. His messaging and affect were motivating, and he tapped into the sense of possibility that comes only with imagination. He became a darling of the left, and the party accepted him as a necessary investment.

In 2024, I watched his campaign sink under the weight of a condition he could not meet. Darling of the left, he could not abandon Palestine. AIPAC poured millions of dollars into 2024's elections to unseat Black and Brown pro-Palestinian candidates and those critical of Israel.* In Bowman's district, just after the October 7, 2023, Hamas attack on Israel, AIPAC had flooded the district with a successful $12 million attack on him.† They portrayed him as "too radical" for the district, and too green. He was neither. Bowman took the same position that a majority of Democrats took: a permanent ceasefire and aid for Gaza. This is hardly radical. AIPAC wanted to punish him for his audacity in standing with Palestine publicly. He never had a chance. It is hard to outrun a PAC with such a large war chest and such effective messaging tactics. AIPAC knew exactly how to organize its communities. AIPAC receives donations from both the Democratic and Republican parties. Yet AIPAC spends a huge fraction of its money on influencing Democratic primaries. How is this possible? How is it possible that in a "democracy," special interest groups backed by wealthy donors have more influence over an election than the voters themselves? Is a functioning democracy a system that can be bought and sold by super PACs and corporate donors? Under these conditions, democracy is simply an investment opportunity for corporations and the superrich. It's hard to feel confident in the voting process when the power of your only tool can be taken away by someone else.

It was in the days after October 7 that I realized I couldn't

---

* Elena Schneider and Melanie Mason, "AIPAC Uncorks $100 Million War Chest to Sink Progressive Candidates," *Politico*, March 3, 2024.

† Michael Arria, "Latimer Defeats Bowman with $15 Million Worth of Help from AIPAC," *Mondoweiss*, June 26, 2024.

see past it. All I could see was Palestine and the centuries of policy that had brought the world to this moment. I'd been voting for this. I had been voting for the perpetuation of legislative decisions that work to annihilate entire races of people, including mine. This was an ontological crisis, a permanent disorientation. Whether I'd vote in the general election felt like a trick question. Could I stomach it?

On Super Tuesday, March 5, 2024, 20 percent of Minnesota voters chose to vote Undecided in the Democratic presidential primary. This was a blaring alarm for the Democratic Party, or at least should have been, but history is what tells us that the party's solipsism kept it from understanding its own vulnerabilities.

Palestine is this empire's Achilles' heel, its full unveiling. From AIPAC to the censuring of Rashida Tlaib, the only Palestinian member of the House, the question of Palestine has highlighted the inconsistencies that mark the failure of the party. Biden's decision to continue to arm Israel and refusal to address the exponentiating understanding that this genocide is not a matter of perception but a matter of near incomprehensible fact. This was a watershed moment when young people especially became engaged with one another about the myriad of ways that the U.S. is an orchestrator of imperialism, colonization, geopolitical crises, and endless warfare. Ironically (or not ironically at all), TikTok, which our government has previously worked to ban; X, owned by the billionaire menace Elon Musk; and Instagram, owned by Facebook, can be thanked in part for this moment of consciousness raising. Young people are increasingly in conversation, educating one another and in the process producing lyrics that reflect their inner world and the way that the outer world complicates that inner world. This base was frustrated with the White House's barefaced complicity and posture, and the generations that decide the future of the party are further distancing themselves from the party. And it makes sense. It makes sense that millennials, and Gen Z, and Gen X, have all come to realize that we are up against a series of impossible choices.

This isn't to say that social progress hasn't happened, and that the vote for Democrats has yielded no practical results. Of course it has. But that progress can be attributed to the pillars of our community who have always had their rights limited to their votes. The success of the civil rights movement can be attributed to the 381-day Montgomery bus boycott and smaller, lesser-known boycotts that hit the state where it hurt most, its economy. In Montgomery, the municipal bus service lost somewhere between $3,000 and $4,000 a day. The withholding of bus fares stifled the local Montgomery market and forced the hand of the local and federal government. In this particularly significant case, it was savvy Black organizers who can be thanked for that historical shift, not the lawmakers who often fail to respond to a need until the entire infrastructure of governance is at risk of falling apart.

When I left my old world and entered this new, more honest world, I found a world in which there would be no need to compromise my ethics or poetics. I left a space of limitations and entered one of abundance, a world of permutations, a world where anything that the poem wants to do, it can do.

"Space" is an active word, a thing that grows and wanes and breaks and invites. In a poem, space is as active as the words that occupy it. In a poem, negative space can become positive space. Space, both the white space that surrounds the words and the white space between the words, confirms for us that we are reading a poem. Space creates rest. Space can be a metaphor; it can also be a concrete boundaried apparatus that controls sound and tells us how to read the poem. Space articulates capacity, space incites the imaginative. Space is a collaboration.

Safia Elhillo says of caesuras, a technique in which space is introduced and emboldened within the line,

> there is silence in them, there is space to be able to rest between stops, walls, closets, even. So, yeah. The caesura is my favorite toy. I'm interested in the hesitation, interested in giving the reader a respite for a second and then going back to the language and what better way than to just have it be silent, to be blank for a second, to get a rest for as long as you want to before moving on to the next chunk of text. And I am not interested in a hard stop, not interested in the hard pause.[*]

Under these violent circumstances, we are being called to rethink our capacity to reimagine what is possible amid the impossible. We are called to resist the impulse to cede power to authoritarianism. We are called to reach for an organized poetics, where the values and functions of poetry should be an organizing principle for future action, a principle that features an aggressive belief that a different world exists for us; an axiom-

---

[*] Safia Elhillo, "Intersections and White Space: An Interview with Safia Elhillo." Interview by Holly Spencer in *The Fourth River*, March, 19, 2019.

atic knowing that the composition of our politics is a manmade concept and is patently godless in its design. Those without the power of the elite are every day exhausted by the many pinpricks of daily life, exhausted and our needs suppressed, and suppression ornaments that exhaustion. Through suppression as a mechanism, the most sinister characters are able to access the poetics of imagination, and they take it as far as they can, imagining worlds in which the rest of us do not even exist, and definitely do not have permission to live.

What has poetry got to do with this?

What hasn't it to do with this?

Poetry facilitates the imaginative work that becomes what Chris Dixon calls "another politics." All of us who go to poetry to construct some small part of a new future are part of this "anti-authoritarian current," in which a "refusal of domination" links activist communities under the commitment to imagine and create new forms of social relation. Where this refusal meets the commitment to imagine, it is poetry and the application of poetics that we can go to as we try to process new anticipations and ways of seeing.

The poem is always political. Even when it is concerned with the abstract and the ineffable. I can write a poem about the transmutation of water into wine, and still the question of whose water and whose wine will remain. Even when the poem is untrue, even when the poem is merely efficient, the question of its fictions and the question of its resolutions are political questions.

Poets often talk about form, both as an aesthetic choice and as a subgenre category. Form is about structure, about organizing, about bringing the reader into the container you've established. Poetry teaches us to invest in forms of evaluation, forms of distillation, forms of care. Form is itself, even if controlled, an example of the way fugitivity can work. Subverting form is a mini exercise in rebellion. Poetry taught me this, yes, but understanding organizing's unique power affirmed it for me.

I'm working with organizations that I understand and trust, with people who are skilled and learned in the brilliant art of movement organizing.

CHAPTER 8

THE OLIVE SEASON

The olive tree is the color of peace, if peace needed
 A color. No one says to the olive tree: How beautiful you are!
 But: How noble and how splendid!
 —Palestinian poet Mahmoud Darwish

In Grenada, my grandfather grows olive trees that line his driveway. It is a luscious house, unbelievable to the eyes of an eight-year-old who had no precedent to judge from. The rats come and steal the olives, climbing the trees in the black of the classic night to gorge on the flesh of the fruit and its pits. Everything and everyone eats the olives, regardless of who the tree belongs to, regardless of the fact that the tree itself is not even native to the land, itself brought to the Caribbean in the 1600s, around the time the people enslaved to till the land were displaced to those shores.

To see the connections among all those elements is political knowledge. That knowledge is sacrosanct. That knowledge is what it takes to reconstruct our origin story and tell a new truth about who we really are as humans and what it means to participate in this dynamic, diverse, animal-dominant world, this world where what is planted, by hand or through language, cannot help but bear its fruit.

It is olive season in Palestine. In the shadow of precious olive trees, the blood of the children of Gaza seeps into the soil. In America, we watch terror rain down on the people of the land and debate their existence, debate their right to safety, debate the fact of our complicity, and still we sleep at night. We sleep as the sun rises on the Palestinian sands, the beaches emptied of their glamor, ships of aid hovering at the ports. We sleep as Palestinian mothers stumble through the rubble of the streets, turning over each body one by one to identify their martyred children, weeping at what they find, weeping for who they will not find, weeping for each other, weeping for themselves. We sleep in the thorny warmth of the West's power. We are not certain that it could never happen to us, but we know that it is unlikely.

In a building bombed into half of itself, a father sets a plate for his children, still young in their innocence. Olives, olive oil, zaatar, and bread. It has taken him days to find this food in the once lush streets of Gaza. Israel has cut the city's water supply, and its power. Israel has bombed the seaports and the borders so that nothing can get in, or out. The hospitals bombed, the boats set aflame, the land petrified in the wake of each blast.

The markets were bombed; the trees too. Across the world, as the fires of Palestine signal to us all, the fruit trees trampled by Israeli forces are being replanted. In colonized lands across the globe, the people have all become gardeners. They are planting the seeds of their ancestors, planting the trees of resistance, planting the trees of connection.

I began with organizing. I began with the politics of bodies, of what it meant to put one's physical being on the line. I began with an investment in direct action, I began with the politics of disruption, I began with agitation. Though I was active, I was nearsighted and didn't really understand the history of organizing, and the impact it has had on the trajectory of history. I wanted immediate satisfaction, I wanted each protest to lead to direct and swift change, I wanted the structures that govern us to hear the cries of genocide and uncover an unknown empathy. I wanted to believe that social change and political change were limbs on the same tree, and that organizing had to work within the bounds of our legislative framework, that organizing and direct action had to augment an "insider" strategy or the marginalized would have no real leverage. But at some point, I realized they weren't.

I came back to organizing with my tail between my legs but with a renewed sense of self. Organizing allows me to put my imagination to use in near unlimited ways, to activate potentials for change in ways that don't require me to ask the permission of the same cruelties that create the conditions we are organizing against.

There are so many more modes of activation and so many more ways to create impact. When we, as Angela Davis says, "demand the impossible," we also denormalize the conditioning that tells us our survival is reliant on how well we can hide ourselves in the genes of the beast.

It turned out that the skills I'd acquired in the belly of the beast taught me what I needed to know to go up against the beast. I had learned how to leverage high-exposure media contacts, how to support a national campaign with tactical strategies that helped propel the messaging of that campaign so that it added to a larger messaging infrastructure. I had learned how to get to people, how to get people to pay attention to their indignations, the things that make it hard for them to hold their heads up. I had learned how to write persuasively, how to synthesize an issue and speak concisely on the merits and significance of an action or a campaign. I was interview-ready, I was TV-ready. I could be ready for a news segment in under an hour, makeup applied and everything.

And unlike elections and electoral campaigns, we win many of our fights. We win when we deliver groceries to a disabled elder, when the workers in our communities unionize, when we pursue narrative intervention, when we tell the stories that need to be told, when we share the information that needs to be shared. We win when our stories about the future feel like poems, when we speak into a new sense of freedom.

We are in the business of winning, because winning is life or death, because we stretch and reshape our people's definitions of the terms "life" and "death," because we are able to transform perceptions of freedom and engage the flourish of ingenuity. In organizing, the wins are wonted and evolving. What a win looks like on a campaign is not what a win looks like when you are among the people you care for and amid the systems of care that sustain your people when the government, the politician, the campaign, and the consultants fail. A win for organizers is getting an institution to redirect funds to those in immediate crisis or feeding a hundred people during a pandemic or endemic siege or getting more books for our libraries. A win for organizers is a win that touches those who don't even believe they need it.

It's not that losing had discouraged me, or that because I lost I feel I need to redeem myself elsewhere. It's that I began to feel that losing was merely the result of a hand played badly, and that winning was random. The cost of losing didn't feel real, it felt compulsive, it stopped feeling like we were fighting for people but instead were fighting for the right to fail them in a host of other ways in order to protect their respective parties.

I felt right again. I felt right using those skills on behalf of the operations that might actually create space in our world for imagination to replace the collective cynicism that allows death-making systems to thrive.

It does not matter what kind of power I have unless it could be a flat kind of power, a circular kind of power, a collective kind of power that touches everything all at once. Fighting for one candidate or one bill or one campaign had worn me down with its tacit mundanity. There were so many issues and so many complicit actors and only so many election seasons and only so many winners.

In April 2022, I attended the White House Correspondents' Dinner—an annual dinner, attended by the president, to celebrate the press and the political elite of D.C.—with a friend and with the hope to build strong connections. We dined, we laughed at the comedian, I socialized with the other Black political operatives and journalists as we grinned and congratulated each other in our nice dresses and good lipsticks and patted ourselves on the back for being good workers of the machine.

The 2022 WHCD took place during my Saturn Return, a period during which it is said that deep transformation happens for a person, a transformation that challenges everything a person may know about themselves, a transformation that taught me how to sit in front of my mirrors. My Saturn Return was preparing me to commit to my alignment, preparing me to pack away doubt and trust what I know and what I had learned about the machinations of the political apparatus. I had no idea just how much I would be transformed within the next year.

October 7, 2023, came, and after it the world was undone, as it should have been. More and more Palestinian people continue to die as I write this, as institutions of all kinds threaten the First Amendment rights of anyone who dares speak or act in support of the Palestinian people and against the genocide of the Palestinian people.

I watched the same Black former colleagues and acquaintances in politics feed the machine by encouraging, airing, trafficking in propagandist talking points. I watched politicians I respected equivocate and prevaricate on the question of genocide. After a graduating college student—who had studied genocide!—was barred from speaking at her commencement, I watched a Black television anchor grill her on whether she supports the abolition of Israel. I watched a Black television anchor say that student protests at universities across the country were antisemitic. I watched them stammer and hem, I watched the light die out from their eyes as the propaganda spilled from their mouths. I watched Rashida Tlaib silenced on the floor of Congress while many of her peers stood by and said nothing. I watched the end of democracy on a big screen, watched the people who once fought for the right to defend democracy in these very spaces become the antithesis to democracy, watched them become the mouthpieces of fascism, watched them participate in the dissolution of the very thing they had demanded entry into. What a waste of spirit. What a waste of mind.

I watched them and asked myself, *What is the point?* What is the point of power, of wanting it, of acquiring it, if we don't use it to attack the most pressing issues of our lifetime? The politician cannot believe that solving infant mortality in the United States is more important than infant mortality in Palestine during an unquestionably genocidal siege unless they believe that what happens in the United States is disconnected from what happens in Israel and in Palestine. The politician can believe that only if their eyes are closed.

I spent the day of the 2024 White House Correspondents' Dinner helping to draft a series of press releases for an action at which activists would gather to protest President Joe Biden and the Western media's complicity in genocide.

Bernie Sanders, who once ran for president and solidified himself as a darling of the left, has neglected to acknowledge that Israel has turned Palestine into an apartheid state, choosing instead to affirm Israel's right to attack Palestine by repeating the ahistorical suggestion that Hamas started "the war" when history tells us clearly that the war began long before October 7, 2023. In 2016, Sanders lambasted Hillary Clinton for refusing to mention the crisis that Palestinians face under occupation. He told Clinton that Israel had the right to defend itself, but that the U.S. needed to abandon a one-sided position on the occupation to recognize Palestinian "dignity." In response to a question about whether or not Israel's attack on Palestine was disproportionate, he said yes, but affirmed that he was "pro-Israel" and that Israel has the right to defend itself from terrorism. He continued to double down on his position on the two-state solution (a position that guarantees Israel's expansion into Gaza and leaves Palestine without any viable approach to true liberation). Then, in the wake of October 7, in response to an attack that was obviously disproportionate, he still maintained that Israel had the "right to defend itself" and refused to call for a ceasefire—despite a seemingly sober (though incorrect) understanding of the "conflict"—until 2025, well after the genocide had claimed hundreds of lives and showed every sign of continuation. These are all stark contradictions. To refuse to name this a genocide, or to name Israel and Zionism as the villains responsible for this genocide, is a slap in the face of justice, and a slap in the face of his supporters who have been shouting for a free Palestine.

That this socialist, leftist, antiwar Democrat known for his anticapitalist platform would refuse to do the simple work of acknowledging a genocide fueled by capitalism, which fuels militarism, is not only a betrayal but a case study. The metonyms of these statements make themselves known. Here, "defend" is used instead of "perpetuate." Here, the word "pro-Israel" is used instead of "Zionist."

Even Sanders cannot escape the compulsions of state-sanctioned violence and the implications of colonialism. Bernie says all the right things to the progressive left. His speeches motivate and enrage. And then, at a 2025 rally in Idaho, in which he once again parroted the claim that Israel has "the right to defend itself," he watched as pro-Palestine activists were removed by police for disrupting his event—an occurrence that he would ostensibly value as a socialist leftist who believes that public dissent is a necessary feature of democracy. Once again, his contradictions bind him. He waited until September 2025, after more than 60,000 Palestinians were killed (a number that is contested, based on systematic underreporting of the death toll) to call the scourge of Palestine a genocide.

We cannot ignore that Sanders's work has influenced voters, and there is no doubt that voters are just a bit more radicalized and more focused on workers' movements because of his influence. This isn't about whether or not he has been good for the country, but rather that being "good for the country" requires that a politician sign on to a list of antithetical compromises that run counter to the ideas of liberation they sell.

Since October 7, hundreds of journalists and media workers have been slaughtered in Palestine. The legacy media class has done little to protect, remember, or even mention these journalists and workers, though they are their colleagues. Legacy media outlets like *The New York Times* have been happy to manufacture consent for this war, trafficking in scurrilous disinformation campaigns (e.g., the debunked[*] story "Screams Without Words") that only further justify the United States' unending financial and narrative support for this genocide.

The WHCD protest, organized mainly by the Palestinian Youth Movement DMV, Dissenters DMV, and the Party for Socialism and Liberation—with support from other entities like Writers Against the War on Gaza, one of the bodies I am fortunate to organize with—drew hundreds of people from across the country and took over the streets outside the Hilton in Washington, D.C., reminding dinner participants of the violence in the fact that the president, administration, and media class of the world were breaking bread and laughing together as they enabled and sanctioned the genocide of Palestinian jour-

---

[*] Jeremy Scahill, Ryan Grim, and Daniel Boguslaw, "'Between the Hammer and the Anvil': The Story Behind the *New York Times* October 7 Exposé," *The Intercept*, February 28, 2024.

nalists whose deaths go unmentioned by their Western colleagues. We hung a Palestinian flag from a window of the Hilton above the U.S. flags flanking the hotel's roundabout. We decorated the ground with PRESS vests splattered with red paint to represent the blood of Palestinian journalists who symbolize the contradictions of Western "freedom." This image was intended to question the validity of a democracy that purports to protect the right to free speech and journalistic freedom celebrating itself as it proves to the world that these are merely concepts, subjective in their composition.

The friend I had accompanied to the dinner two years earlier was at this dinner, and on her Instagram I had a window into the world I'd left behind. The sense of déjà vu made an appearance. At that moment, it felt inevitable that I had ended up on this side of the phone, looking in from outside the Hilton rather than looking out from the inside. It reminded me of the significance of my little personal revolution. There was a line, there were two sides. On one side was the performance of change. On the other side was the vehicle of it.

Organizing showed to me again the immanent mechanisms of humanness. How could I have lost faith in the thing that makes belonging the lifeblood that it is? Organizing is the connective tissue that brings imagination and concrete action into practice. Organizing is how we create the telephone of ideas, that endless, iterative list that all worlds are born from.

Imagination derives from the Latin verb *imaginari*, meaning "to picture oneself." Images and language of thought help us see what has not yet been seen, what is not yet there. Aristotle described imagination as "that in virtue of which an image occurs in us," as though imagination is a department of the self in which the self and the world around it are produced by whatever images the self can conjure. The image abstracts the thought, and the thought abstracts the image, abstracting reason, remaking (but not undoing) it all. That imagination can mean the difference between a forty-minute commute to work and a twenty-minute commute to work, or the difference between well-funded schools and dated curriculums for our kids.

A poetic education is premised on the assumption of creative agency, on the idea that each reader has the ability to imagine illusion, to see illusion, to articulate illusion. The training is in learning to qualify it within the line. Said famously by James Baldwin in his book *Nobody Knows My Name: More Notes of a Native Son*, "This illusion owes everything to the great American illusion that our state is a state to be envied by other people: we are powerful, and we are rich. But our power makes us uncomfortable and we handle it very ineptly. The principal effect of our material well-being has been to set the children's teeth on edge. If we ourselves were not so fond of this illusion, we might understand ourselves and other peoples better than we do, and be enabled to help them understand us."* The poet is the first to understand that safety is an illusion that power constructs. We learn through metaphor. For instance, in Atlanta a man self-immolated in front of the Israeli embassy. Police showed up at

---

* James Baldwin, *Nobody Knows My Name: More Notes of a Native Son* (Dial Press, 1961).

the scene almost instantly. They pointed guns at him while onlookers cried out for water. They pointed their guns at him as he was burning alive. This image says more words about safety than I can afford. He was unarmed. He posed a threat only to himself in an act of protest. The police pointed their guns at him as he protested for life with his life. This image is a metaphor for the way imperial colonial power pervades every inch of American democracy.

When we organize we are taking imagination beyond its limits, attempting to materialize, through the strength of numbers, what has been made impossible by a few. We approach the poetic in order to articulate those realities that we organize against, we can go to poetry to mark the design of the world we see and the world we desire to conjure. In the labor movements of the thirties, the civil rights movement of the sixties, and the Grenadian revolution of 1979, the poem has always been a collaborator in the work of creating and sustaining movements. Books in general have the power to do this, but poetry most uniquely asks us to imagine the surreal, to imagine the hyperreal, and to help us organize and identify the complexity of emotions that make every moment an organizing moment.

It matters, though, that community organizers are the ones who can help shape those choices at the local and federal levels so that community wins center people's most pressing daily needs. The wins, then, are not partisan, but personal. Every person is touched by the current of the win when the win is personal.

I learned some of this later than I should have, but it doesn't take away from the fact that I had to. It was inevitable. I am the child of organizers who have fought against imperial regimes for most of their lives, putting their bodies on the line against the connecting oppressions that shaped their world and the world we inherited from them. Eventually I would have to confront the world I'd been running away from and the responsibility that is my birthright. Perhaps it's because I didn't want to sacrifice anything, or maybe that I wasn't ready to.

What I know about the world is cumulative. I take each fact I learn and build on it with a new fact, building and building until I begin to see the shape of the problem, like a puzzle. Often, at the start of a puzzle, you have pieces floating astray in the outline because their place hasn't yet been revealed. Sometimes my collection of knowledges feels like rash splatters of matter floating with me. Then I stumble on that one piece, that one missing magnetic link, that pulls all these floating, isolated facts together, clarifying the image. That happens with time. That happens with the humility that comes after you realize you're wrong, which also takes time to develop, which is an unending project for me. I had to find out through experience that I had been thinking wrongly. I had to trust that the intuitive nature that was waking up inside me existed in others, had to let myself be inspired by the thinkers who came before me to be truly brave in my intellectual ambitions. It's one thing never to have invested in power in the first place—it's another to accumulate power and then realize too late that you must divest.

In every part of the world, someone is whispering in the ear of someone else that justice is near and that the fight is upon them. In every part of the world, someone is pursuing the activation of imagination on behalf of everyone else.

In the poem (or song, or both) "The Revolution Will Not Be Televised," written by then teenage college student Gil

Scott-Heron, we are offered a praxis. We are told that revolution requires something practical of us, that we cannot participate passively, that we cannot be lured by the images of change that are being sold to us, that it has to come from somewhere inside, that it has to be cultivated in the privacy of one's mind.

"So when we said the revolution would not be televised," Heron told filmmaker Skip Blumberg in 1991, "we were saying that, like, the thing that's gonna change people is something that no one will ever be able to catch on film, it'll just be something that you see and all of a sudden you'll realize 'I'm on the wrong page,' or 'I'm on the right page but I'm on the wrong note and I've got to get in sync with everyone else to understand what's happening in this country.'"*

Our job, as poet thinkers, is to hypostatize the imaginary, to ask the poem to say what we need it to say, to be the ones to proclaim freedom and to document it and then to get in sync with the other thinkers and imaginaries who need to be with each other to build the mass movements that create change and usher in peace. The poem can be a peaceful poem when it needs the reader to find peace. But peace can be unsettling too, which the poem can capture.

I started teaching college students in both undergraduate and graduate study in 2023. This was full circle for me—I had started by teaching young students how to write, both critically and creatively, during my time at Harlem Children's Zone. Those same students would have been in graduate school by the time

---

* Gil Scott-Heron. Interview by Skip Blumberg, *The 90's*, PBS, 1989.

I started teaching in higher education. It was as if I had grown into this profession, as if everything about me led to this.

In the fall semesters of 2023 and 2024, I taught a class called Rites of Passage, originally taught by the poet, teacher, singer, and activist Sekou Sundiata in 1988. The class asked my undergraduate students to "consider the role of the Challenge, the Vision Quest and the Initiation in rites of passage." These are all stages of awakening in which the subject is able to chart her evolution and map out a vision for the future that will guide her in her life's work.

In my classrooms, especially in my poetry workshops, I ask my students to write a sonnet for the end of the world. The most literal thinkers approach the prompt apocalyptically. They want to write about romance in the face of war, about the blue wraith of gun smoke. I have no expectations when I offer this prompt—there is no right answer—and I wouldn't tell them even if I did, but always there is a poem with a turn at the end that begins the poem anew, or a poem fixated on incorporeal death with a turn that comes alive, and I am always delighted to hear it, to see it, to live in the imagination of a poem that wants to be somewhere other than where it is. It is an ungovernable poem, a poem outside its limits, a poem outside the poet's limits, an adynaton.

When I ask them to imagine the end of the world, I am asking them to practice a kind of ungovernability, to pursue an ending—or beginning—that abandons conventionality and seeks a turn that is inherently unfamiliar, ugly in its rarity. The poems that stick with me most are the poems about wrestling freedom away from a predetermined fate, about surviving the end, about living again. By imagining a world that departs from this one, they are choosing to shape how the future might look and work and choosing to determine their own fates, their own deaths, their own chances to come alive again.

We are doing this work of imagining from within the project of the academy. We are, by simply engaging with the experiment of imagination, challenging the academy's resistance to play, resistance to desystemizing discovery. Doing this kind of work requires the urgency of ungovernability, and requires that we challenge the constraints of the project in order to escape its insistence on order and the replication of order.

My role as a professor is not to guide, but to make space for self-guidance. My job is to teach my students to think for themselves. So when they write, I am asking them to consider the ending as the beginning. I am asking them to investigate and approach nonlinearity as a way to consider how history functions—in literature and, naturally, in the present of our lives.

What does a poet have, and what does the poem allow for the poet? It allows for flight, for departure, for return. It allows for the defamiliarization and disruption of the factory of everyday language, and the factories of rhetoric. When I ask the end a question about the beginning, language returns to me a fact. When I ask a question about ambition, poetry responds with possibility. This is true for the good poets, and the bad poets—we set the terms of freedom.

We are well past the days of encampments in universities across the country as I write this, and well into the days of a terrifying but familiar episode of authoritarian repression in which students are being abducted in plain sight by a fascist regime headed up by Donald Trump. Following threats of federal funding cuts, universities like Columbia, which receives most of its funding via endowments, have begun to concede to the demands of the Trump administration, which include empowering campus security to arrest students and to change the leadership and function of the Institute for Israel and Jewish Studies and the international affairs school to address unsubstantiated and baseless claims of antisemitism from pro-Palestinian and anti-imperialist activists. Journalists on the ground in Palestine, who have been systematically exterminated by the Israeli military, risked their lives and the lives of their families to tell these stories. And they were targeted because they were able to offer to the world narratives that tell the truth about what is happening on the ground in Gaza. Their commitment is not just a reflection of their integrity but a reflection of their commitment to the Palestinian movement for liberation. And their steadfast commitment has had an infectious influence on the work of U.S. student journalists and student activists across the country who work day and night to tell the stories on the ground, stories that defeat the claims of the fascist imperialist state. It's those same students who've been combating mainstream media's complicity, who have been doubling down on competing narratives that highlight Palestinian resistance, who have been reshaping the stories that the world is being told about Palestine. I saw these students write some of the best press releases I'd ever seen in the entire decade of my political work. I've seen them give interviews that are more strategic and more compelling than all the interviews I'd done in the entire decade of my political work. Not only do I honor these students, but I recognize the poetics of their praxis. It is rooted in an understanding that language can tell the truth, or it can tell a lie. The poem is an empty slate, void, until we decide its intention. What the poets do with that neutrality is good. They make the point of poetry good. The political is personal. And the personal is poetry.

The colonizer's poetry has no bones next to the lyric of ours.

In the backyard of my grandmother's home, a passion fruit tree grows, its fruit falling with the weight of a small apple; in its insides, however, the taste of something yearningly tropical and godly. It grows deliberately, without permission, nourishing itself with its waste, with the song of the sun, with the rainwater of hungry, earthly complexity, with the fact of its long life. "You know what this is?" My uncle stands above me, holding a spoon to the open cup of the fruit. I shake my head. "It's passion fruit. It grows right back there, on our land. You can eat it."

At the end of the world is a freedom that begins in the mind.

British White Paper of June 1922

███████████████████████████████████
███████████████████████████████████
██████████ Palestine ██████████████
███████████████████████████████████
███████████████████████████████████
███████████████████████████████████
████████
████ which has prevailed ██████████
███████████████████████████████████
███████████████████████████████████
███████████████████████████████████
████████████████████
███████████████████████████████████
██████████████ is ████████████████
███████████████████████████████████
████████████████████ the upbuilding of
████████
███████████████████████████████████
███████████████████████████████████
███████████████████████████████████
████ change.
████████ three generations ████████
████████████ work ████ the land. This community
has its own political organs ██████████

LET THE POETS GOVERN - 167

its distinctive intellectual life

its own language, its own customs, its own life, When it is asked what is meant

it become a centre and a pride

That is why it is necessary that the existence of Palestine should be guaranteed, and that it should be formally recognized to rest upon ancient historic connection.

This, then, is the interpretation

upon this basis may be built up that a spirit of cooperation must largely depend.

CHAPTER 9

THE FOURTH SERMON ON THE WARPLANE, OR THE CODA

AFTER GWENDOLYN BROOKS
AFTER LILLIAN-YVONNE BERTRAM

It is fall, and with my wife, I weave my body between the trees of the orchard. I plan to make apple pie, applesauce, apple cider. How to make comes to me intuitively. How to make lives in the lines of my palm. In the orchard, just days after the U.S. formally descended into regression, I sit among the sweetness of the apple's nectar and realize that the end of the world is coming. There is little left to look forward to, little to rejoice in. But when I sit in this orchard with the people I love, with the community I've submitted my labor to, I feel hope waiting for me. We are all in the orchard, making use of the apple in as many ways as we can. And of course, fear and despair sit with us too.

We all fear the ache of knowledge, that sensory data that articulates our nature. We crave innocence, the shield that deadens our senses and lessens the labor and lightens the heavy load of knowledge. This antagonism is replicated in generation after generation, a nutrient in the soil. But we learned to survive this enmity, dressing it up with rituals, using it to realize our spirituality, to realize continuity. We are both resentful of the apple and ravenous for its seductive flavor, its satiating gifts.

Humans make record of the harvest, we make art with the flesh of the fruit, make marks with the black of the seed, we infect the world with this nameless hunger so that we will always yearn for what has been lost in the burning of the trees, so that they will always feel the pull of the fruit, so that they may remember their subdued impulses, that generative urge to sow.

This is recordkeeping. This recordkeeping is poetry. That urge to sow is what gives birth to poetry: the yearning for language to animate that record, that flesh, that seed. This is bravery, that step one takes in between thinking and marking. The poem is a thought made up of images and language. The mark making is the visualization of speech, of language. The poem preceded itself. The poem had already found its speaker.

We have written hundreds of thousands of fantasies about the end of the world. We have written hundreds of movies about the end of the world. Intentionally and without intention, we mocked the end until it came hungering after us. We imagined war, zombies (dead humans who were still alive, go figure), and we imagined an asteroid event, and we imagined death by nuclear weapon. We imagined redemption of the good, elimination of the evil. We imagined that some of us would be protected from the wrath of the earth's nature. This too was poetry. These are the images conjured by someone's imagination of the end of the world, the images that the rest of us rely on to understand what the end of the world actually is.

In the end, there was no good, and there was no evil. The end of the world is the end of what we knew, the beginning of a new origin story, a new version of us. The end of the world is a return to the principles that guide our survival: reciprocity, community, and mutuality.

Some say that history is no evidence of what could happen in the future, but this couldn't be further from the truth. What we do in the past is likely what we will do in the future unless learning occurs. Unless we change our minds when new learning occurs. Unless we are dedicated to the task of righteousness and what it requires. We must fight to receive what we have inherited. As in, if the earth decides we still fit into its ecosystem of health, then we must commit ourselves to its nature, to its fundamental needs, to our implicit agreement. It means that we do not poison the oxygen we must all breathe, that we do not define the earth by the harms we create. The earth is not resisting; we are failing to understand our responsibility to it. The whales are not "rebelling," we are failing to understand our relationship to them.

Earning our keep is about reciprocity. It is about respecting the absolute privilege of living in a rich world, a world that gives great ease to the needs of humans, that provides everything a human needs: water, food, housing, community, pleasure, light, warmth. What we know about the living world is already enough to establish a relationship of mutuality, of generosity and investment, of care.

Early creation myths and origin stories give us clues into the early poetics of human nature and the human experience. They do more than express the beliefs of particular religions—they give us insight into the motifs that guide the collective experience of human expression. These motifs illustrate for us what early humans believed they needed in order to live meaningful lives. First, it shows us that early humans wanted to find meaning. They wanted to feel that their place in the universe was of significance, they wanted to understand why they were created, wanted a sense of order to help them understand their relationship to the earth. Second, these motifs show us that early humans searched for profundity. It shows that regardless of origin, human beings have always been asking the same questions about humanity, about pain, about grief. It shows that they were in search of catharsis, of a way to relieve the pain of the cycle of life, to comprehend death and loss, of a way to feel without grief being all-consuming. They wanted to produce something from grief, to create figures out of grief, to make monuments to honor it, to remind themselves of the relationship between heart and body, mind and soul. Grief is as transcendent as pleasure, and poetry is as compulsive as healing. They work together to help the human being understand its humanity. That is the unique power of living a poetic life.

Most origin stories start at the beginning, with human birth, because this is where our lives begin, where our consciousness begins. But what if the creation story began at the end? What if what makes us is what ends us, what if the human life cycle is not a series of beginnings but a series of endings—would we think differently about mortality? Would we think differently about the machinations of time? Would we replace our focus on the beginnings—the beginnings of humanity, the beginning of consciousness—with a focus on the end and the future? Would we redefine ourselves and our ecological relationship through frameworks of desire versus negation?

We suffer amnesia. We forget history at the expense of the future. We forget to name the crisis.

But the human exists to tell stories. We think with words. We govern our lives with language. Our thinking matters. The words we think with matter. Our reflections matter, even when we are looking into a glass we don't own.

We are the cultivators of the birth of consciousness, the cultivators of a soil rich with purpose. We plant and sow and grow more apple trees than they can burn. We are born and reborn in the mulch. Born and reborn in the orchard. The artist is the farmer. But the poem is the buried seed.

Despair is simple, it lacks complexity, it exhausts itself. At some point, you must conjure. At some point, you must eat. I am not a cynic, but a poet. What else is there to do but reach for poetics to understand despair? Even in the face of despair, even in the face of unimaginable power, what else is there to do but resist?

I have retraced my footsteps to find the moments when I have changed and was changed by being a political worker. I regret none of it and do not feel compelled to apologize for any of it. Every decision I made, every choice I made within the allowances of language, brought me to this orchard. I have been offered a profound amount of luck. I understand that the idea of luck can be reductive, as it presumes that a person with luck has success only by happenstance. But I do think that this is true in my case. I came from little, but in the process of becoming the person who writes to you right now, I have myself become part of the privileged class. I write books. I can feed myself and my family. I live in a comfortable home unweathered by the trauma of my childhood. I did not earn this, I was allowed this. Talent is an exceptional tool, but no person *is* exceptional. In some ways, I am capitalizing on the devastation of our political condition. I get to write about it, to intellectualize it, to dream up arguments against it, and I am being paid to give you this argument. But I am, hopefully, earning my keep in the world by offering thoughts that highlight the exigency of the undercommons. I add myself to that universe of thought to make meaning of what I've learned, to make sure that I pass that learning on to someone else. I spend my life thinking because that is greater than any single action I can take. I spend my life thinking and making material of that thinking because I am a poet. That's all being a poet really is.

If you're reading this, it means that this story has survived the end, that this book has escaped the rubble. If you're reading this, that means you have entered the orchard. If you're reading this, then you already know the apperceptive cost of hunger. You've learned how to make, how to knead, and how to work the science of yeast and sugar.

I was afraid to write this poem, given the heat, given the threat of language and the threat of what it can do. I am no martyr, but in the process of speaking to you I have died many times and have been rebirthed in the same breaths. I know so little, and what I know I offer to you, I entrust to you, dear reader, dear holder of the future, dear holder of the past. What I know today is different from what I'll know tomorrow, or next month, or in a decade, if I'm to last that long. I hope that you'll allow me the grace of contradiction, that you'll see the me of this moment and be able to reconcile it with the me of the future. I promise to write to you again, to tell you everything I know about change, how it happened, how it didn't, what's left for you to complete.

Though there was much destruction, I want you to know that there was so much love. I want you to know that those of us standing in the orchard brought more of us into the orchard, because we loved on our people, because we would not abandon them. We organized our people. We made sure that even under the impossible weight of a rising fascism, we were able to save some lives and save some minds. We sat together in the bare sun of the day and then again in the shade of the night to fight for each other. I was afraid. I wanted the solution to come quickly.

But then I realized that my job is not to politick, it is not to perform. My job is to ask questions. This is the role of the poet. The poet organizes their world by tilling the soil. They harvest, eat, and return the seeds to the land, until they do it all over again. The poet locates the fact of the undercommons and dilates the eye to see only what is fugitive, only what breaks away from the page to enter the reader.

But nothing worth pursuing comes quickly. Restructuring our society, reconsidering our democracy, is not an overnight project. That's why the project belongs to you, because for now I have exhausted my capacity, because I have said all I came to say.

Most origin stories begin at the beginning. But now you know that the exit is on the way in. May the apple plant its seed through all of eternity. Get up from your sorrowful slumber. Get up and eat. This is the great migration of the now. The origin story begins at the end.

ERASURE OF AMERICAN SONNET 91 BY WANDA COLEMAN

mercy

bent

a wing

not without   pleasure,

as the body organized itself against the will

of   chronic seeings

was't hunger or holiness spurred the sighting?

ACKNOWLEDGMENTS

This book has changed my life, and I offer great thanks to those who have inspired it and those who have supported me through this process, even when it was at its most trying. Thank you to my agent, Alice Whitwham, whose vision and support encourage and protect me. Thank you to my editor, Nicole Counts, who believed in this book and accepted its pivots. Thank you to the many hands who have touched the many drafts of this book, including Chanda Prescod-Weinstein, Claire Potter, Jace Clayton, and my dad.

Thank you to Fred Moten, the first to tell me "You are the only one who can write this book," and to Pato Herbert, who inspired me to change my mind. Thank you to Kiese Laymon, whose endless support inspired me to be brave in the making of this work.

And to my community—Gb Kim, Mahogany L. Browne, Jason Reynolds, Joselia Hughes, Christine Platt—thank you for being everything I needed.

I also owe my gratitude to the many voices, living and dead, who haunt these pages, including George Jackson, Mahmoud Darwish, M. NourbeSe Philip, Sylvia Wynter, James Baldwin, and an endless list of more.

ABOUT THE AUTHOR

CAMONGHNE FELIX, poet and essayist, is the author of *Dyscalculia: A Love Story of Epic Miscalculation*, which was hailed by *Time* and *Vogue* as one of the most anticipated books and top memoirs of 2023. Her poetry debut, *Build Yourself a Boat*, was long-listed for the 2019 National Book Award in Poetry and short-listed for the Lambda Literary Awards. Her poetry has appeared in *Academy of American Poets, Harvard Review, LitHub, The New Yorker, Poetry Magazine, Freeman's,* and elsewhere. She teaches creative writing at The New School in New York City.

X: @camonghne
Instagram: @camonghne